From Where I Sit

FROM WHERE I SIT

by Bill Zalot

DEDICATION

This is not a complete collection of my body of work as a writer. It is but a mere sample. However, I hope all who read these reflections are blessed by them. The collection is dedicated with love to the memory of my Dad and Mom who were always there for me.

It is also dedicated to my family and all who have helped me in my faith journey. Without their support I couldn't have been a living puppet for the Lord all these years. They have been my legs, my arms and transportation. They have helped me to soar on eagle's wings and often have been the wind beneath my wings.

Lastly, I want to dedicate this collection of writings to the editors who through the years have considered what I have written from a perspective most people seldom recognize or consider a valid voice. God has given me an ability to put down my thoughts on paper. I pray the selections I have chosen honor Him!

CONTENTS

FOREWORD
By Mike Aquilina

I first knew Bill Zalot as a series of voice-mails. It was 1996, and I'd just taken the editorship of *New Covenant* magazine. In the stretch of time between editors, the messages had gone unchecked. Bill was calling to check up on manuscripts he submitted. When he didn't get a response, he called again. And again. I called him first, of course.

How could I do otherwise? His messages had the ring of the Gospel about them. It's the voice that makes bold and persists, even after everyone else has told him to give up. "Lord, that I may see!" "Lord, help me ... even the dogs eat the crumbs that fall from their masters' table." "I believe. Help my unbelief!"

Such are the voices that get attention, from God or man.

Bill got my attention. I can't remember whether I accepted the manuscript he was inquiring about in those voice-mails, but I accepted many others. In the years I served as editor of *New Covenant* (1996-2002), Bill's byline appeared often in the magazine. I looked for material that was personal, practical, and anecdotal, and that's precisely what Bill produced. I'm proud to notice that many of the essays in this collection originally appeared in the pages of *New Covenant*.

They have a voice and a perspective that are distinctively Bill's. Having lived a half-century in a wheelchair, he's viewed life from an angle far different from my own. He's caught much that I've missed. Through his writing, he's helped me overcome my disability and see the world as he sees it, from where he sits.

God creates each of us with just the right measure of abilities and disabilities, physical, mental, emotional, professional, situational. Every life comes with limits. The limits help to define us, but not in a deterministic way. When we face a high wall on one side, we have many options. We can sit before it and feel sorry for ourselves. Or we can find a creative way to get over it — or bring it down. Or we can wheel around and move in a direction that gives us more room to roam.

Bill has faced the walls, and he's tried all the options. That's what makes his stories work.

Sometimes he's the hero, Rambo in a motorized wheelchair, speaking out against injustice. Sometimes he lets shame or stubbornness or self-pity get the better of him. It's all there in these candid essays.

Bill's disability is particular, but his story is universal because he's a true storyteller. Spastic cerebral palsy has given him a wealth of experiences, which are a writer's stock in trade. He's known failure, frustration, rejection, vulnerability, dependence, insults, humiliation … as well as deep friendship, unique professional opportunities, the necessity of hard work, and the call to self-giving service. He's been able to pray for people, counsel them, and call them to account. His prayers and his counsel are efficacious, because he doesn't just talk the talk. He wheels the walk.

Bill's disability has been enabling, even empowering. This should not surprise anyone who professes Christianity. When Jesus preached the Beatitudes, he turned the cosmic order on its head, blessing the poor and those who mourn while cursing those who have their ease. Most of us get this in theory, and we nod assent. Bill knows it in his limbs and in his needs. His mother taught him well when she told him he was a benefactor, not merely a beneficiary, when he called out for help and let others assist him. He gives them an opportunity to serve, to encounter Christ (see Matthew 25:37-40), to imitate Christ, and so to become Christ.

This book belongs to everyone who suffers with disabilities, and that means all of us. From his unusual angle Bill shows us our own lives afresh. In his experience, we see our own, perhaps for the first time.

ACKNOWLEDGEMENTS

There are so many people I want to thank for making this book possible. The first is Mike Aquilina who first gave me national exposure in a monthly periodical, *New Covenant* Magazine. His connection gave me a priceless number of contacts with *Our Sunday Visitor* and its various publications.

I would also like to thank Father Mike Scanlon, whose advice was "share the gift of your disability as part of faith experience. Through it, you connect to readers from a unique perspective." Prior to that chance meeting in New Orleans, LA in 1987, I barely noted my disability at the end of a cover letter, let alone in a feature I was writing. Taking his advice has empowered my writing and ability to share my Catholic faith in a dynamic way.

My writing developed with help and support of men like the late C. Edmond Hopper who saw my potential in his special education class. His belief in me also opened the door to mainstreaming. This brings me to Mr. Robert Soderblom. This special man allowed me to write my one and only screenplay. It was produced for our 7th grade social studies class on a super eight movie projector. Only thing I remember about the project is that I played a judge. I recall banging a big gavel giving me a real sense of power.

Lastly, I want to thank my "Venus in Blue Jeans" who has tirelessly helped me select and edit the features for this book. Without her encouragement and continuous support, this project wouldn't have gotten off the ground.

This grateful heart thanks one and all!

A STORY OF SACRIFICE

My Dad was born June 30, 1924 in Philadelphia, Pa. He had 13 brothers and sisters. The former Anna Mae Keating was born January 1, 1927. An only child, Mom was raised by a sister of her mom who had several children of her own. Mom considered this aunt's children as her brothers and sisters. We children saw these people as our aunts and uncles; and we called this Aunt Grandmom Wingate.

On January 31, 1948, these two individuals were married. They will celebrate their forty-fifth wedding anniversary next January—God willing. In that time they have had many trials. In 1975, dad suffered a heart attack. This heart condition forced him to retire at age 51.

In December 1981, a bypass was required for dad. It was successful and dad lives an active life. In 1954, on June 27, I, William J. Zalot, was born three days prior to his thirtieth birthday. I, Bill, the third of nine children, have spastic cerebral palsy, and need a wheelchair for mobility. I am the second of five sons. He and mom are parents of four daughters, and grandparents to seven grandchildren, with a grand-child due in September. Despite his age, he virtually is my arms and legs. He bathes me, shaves me, dresses me and takes care of my personal needs.

Our parents are our first teachers. Our relationship and view of God Our Father, depends a great deal on our relationship and view of our earthly father. If he is someone whose lap we can curl up on, then we will have a healthy relationship with our heavenly Father.

When the story of our father's life, Walter J. Zalot, Sr., a 68-year-old from Levittown, Pennsylvania, is written, it will be highlighted by his personal acts of personal sacrifice and devotion to the well being of his family. For much of his life he held down two jobs to keep food on our table. We children always had clothes on our bodies and food in our stomachs.

Dad's main job was being a milkman. He worked odd hours, leaving the house at 2 or 3 am six days a week. On Saturdays he got home at 5 pm. He often had to take one or more of us (for there were nine of us) to the doctors, for mom never learned to drive.

Some of his second jobs included: being a

salesman at a department store, working with a carpenter, an exterminator—just to name a few. We children never heard of his personal sacrifice, but we knew if we needed anything, we would get it, regardless of the cost. There is a clear distinction between *need* and *want*. Yet, dad did see that each of us who could attend Catholic School did so. I was the only child that never attended Parochial School. I attended CCD classes.

Our parents have lived a simple faith. Dad's brother, Uncle Frank, lived in our home for nearly 20 years, until his death in 1977. Cousins have stayed with us to get away from the city streets in the summer. Our home has always been a haven for the neighborhood. I cannot recall someone in need ever being turned away. Even today children consider our home their second home, and this type of welcome continues to this day.

Today, his grandchildren, our nieces and nephews, feel the warmth of his welcome to our home. One nephew Travis, 10, arrives at our home at 7 am to be fed and looked after before school and returns here in the afternoon after school. Our dad, his grandfather, often takes him to his baseball practice or his "Little League" games.

Travis is my late brother Joe's son. He lives with his mom, our sister-in-law Cathy, but spends a great deal of his time at our home. Our parents have taken him under their wings, showing him love and compassion; as have my sister Cathy and brother-in-law Bill; where Travis has spent many of his weekends, since Joe's death.

In his sacrifice, in his living, in his sharing, in his loving, we who know him, see a glimpse of our heavenly Father's love. For nearly forty-five years, our parents have been married dad has been the provider. This reflection, has been written in a Spirit of Thanksgiving. For our father, and all the fathers out there, who live lives of sacrifice, Happy Father's Day!

MY ARMS, MY LEGS, MY HERO

*The story of a father's
sacrificial love for his disabled son*

S hortly before my Father's death in March of 2001, I found a T-shirt at the bottom of my dresser drawer—the shirt that my family told me aptly described the type of relationship I had with my father. The discovery took me back to a summer by the sea many years ago and opened the floodgates to a host of memories. Those memories were shared over the last few months of Dad's life. During that time, my Mom, Dad and I began most our days with a visit from a Eucharistic Minister. This went on until days before dad's death on March 17, 2001.

I am the third oldest of nine children and was born with spastic cerebral palsy. Throughout my life, I was always physically dependent on my father. Dad was thirty years my senior. Throughout much of my life dad was my arms and legs. I have always needed others to bathe, shave, and dress me. For most of my life, dad took the responsibility for that care.

One year while our family vacationed at the New Jersey shore, my brothers and sisters bought me a shirt that said it well: "When I'm in trouble, I call Dad!" The gag gift really hit me hard. Reflecting on my total dependency on my father, I seldom used the shirt. As I have often said, "Who needs a constant reminder of one's dependency on anyone all day long?"

However, I eventually came to realize, after much thought, "In many ways we all need these reminders." My disability has allowed me to recognize our heavenly Father in my dad's actions each day. I state with conviction, "The reality is that none of us could so much as lift a finger if God didn't give us the ability to do so."

My Invincible Dad

Like many kids, I grew up believing that my father was invincible. In my eyes, Dad was a hero. Although I couldn't play baseball myself, dad made sure that I felt a part of my brothers' Little League teams. I laugh as I recall this thought, "I often brought a building block to the baseball game and pretended to broadcast the game. The block was my microphone, and my brothers and most of their teammates humored my role-playing as I interviewed key players after each game." Continuing my recollection, "Dad knew that this role-playing was a great way to develop my language skills and speech."

As a child, I hoped to become the next Vince Scully, the sports announcer who anchored major league baseball's "Game of the Week" on the NBC television network for many years. Dad coached my brothers' teams when he could, and for many of those games, he dragged me, his disabled son, along. Eventually, my grandmother brought me a tape recorder, which I took to these games and continued to "broadcast."

My father enjoyed watching baseball on TV, but he wasn't too enthusiastic about driving to Philadelphia to watch the major league games in the ballpark. I remember, "Both the limited parking and the crowds bothered dad."

This is why I will never forgot one occasion when I was ten years old; it was the summer of 1964. Philadelphia Phillies that fall would break the hearts of every Philly fan young and old alike as they lost the National League Pennant by one game to the St. Louis Cardinals. The Cards won 93 games and lost 69, while the Phillies finished the season with 92 wins and 70 losses.

Nonetheless, this is the story of one game that summer which illustrated a Dad's unconditional love and sacrifice for his family. It is not about the fact that the team lost a 6 and 1/2 game lead with 12 games remaining in the season.

Dad had purchased tickets for the family to attend a Phillies game that summer. Late that season the day arrived to use the purchased tickets. Our seats were high above in the top row of the stadium, and I recall with love and amazement 44 years later, "Dad, physically carried me to my designated seat. I wore braces on my legs then, and it couldn't have been easy for him to carry me that high."

In telling this story I must conclude by saying," this was just another example of the sacrifices he routinely made for me and the rest of the family." My eyes sparkle as I recall this memory. I hope the enthusiasm which I have in sharing this story matches the warmth in my heart by telling it.

Lastly, the day of Dad's funeral, March 22, 2001 our Blessed Lord gave me a rare privilege. I, the disabled son whom he covered nightly, pulled the blanket to my father's shoulders before his coffin was closed and we celebrated a Mass of Christian burial for this loving husband, father of nine, and now grandfather of 16, great-grandfather of one, uncle, brother and friend to so many. At least on that day, I finally saw our roles reverse.

The third Sunday in June is Father's Day. It has given me pleasure to share this story with you, my readers, and wish all the men who take on the role of Father a "Happy Father's Day!"

ROUTINE SACRIFICES

Mom celebrated her eightieth birthday on January 1, 2007 and she died three days later on January 4, 2007. On January 9, 2007 we celebrated this remarkable woman's life with a Mass of Christian burial. She is a mother of nine and grandmother of 15. Her name is Anna Mae Zalot. On this Mother's Day, I pay tribute to her.

I am the third of nine children. If that doesn't tell one that Mom loved children, then the fact that she babysat countless numbers through the years should. For she never made much money on her efforts due to the fact that our Mom often fed those children who were in her care several meals a day. It seemed Mom's kitchen never closed. I often said, "Mom, you are the best cook ever!" I think I saw "the multiplication of the loaves and fish" take place in our home on more than one occasion. Mom knew how to stretch a meal. No matter who dropped by, they were always welcomed to dine with us.

She welcomed cousins and even an uncle who needed a "temporary home." In my uncle's case the situation ended 20 years later with his death. Mom and Dad always welcomed the stranger and there was none stranger than our Uncle Frank. He lived with us from 1956 until his death in 1976. His temporary stay certainly earned our Mom brownie points toward her eternal reward.

For 53 years Mom and Dad were married from January 31, 1948 until Dad's death on March 17, 2001. In that time they were role models for Christian marriage to our family, the Church and community which were everything to them. What my Mom and Dad couldn't give to the Church financially, they gave to the Church in volunteer time. This was especially true during the two weeks each summer at Saint Mike's fair.

Faith never took a vacation, whether we went to the Jersey Shore, Chicago or Alabama we always attended Mass. It was the focal point of our week. Praying the Rosary daily as a family was also a part of the fabric of our lives as Catholics.

But to think that faith was all that our lives as a family was based on is a mistake for Mom was passionate about the Phillies. She was a loyal fan. Mom lived and died through many losing seasons. Too often Mom had to settle for the refrain "wait until next year!" and that loyalty was rewarded in 1980 when a scrappy bunch of veterans and unknowns sat atop the baseball world.

Mom was as loyal to our endeavors as she was to that baseball franchise from Philadelphia. She worked the concession stand or watched many baseball or softball games my brothers or sisters took part in.

Regardless of the activity Mom was there for us. Whether it was our school plays, a baseball or a softball game or a PTA meeting Mom was there. She was there for us on big days and small. We received consolation for a failure or loss as well as congratulations for the smallest of successes.

What Mom and Dad couldn't contribute financially to the Church, they gave in their effort and time. This was especially true with their work at the Church's annual fair. Mom continued those efforts after Dad's death.

Family gatherings like picnics were big events. Mom made tons of potato salad over the years to nothing but raves and cheers. While Dad grilled franks, burgers and chicken to a crisp. With a swing set, slide and an above-ground-pool summer parties were a hit. They were some of the same reasons our backyard was a neighborhood magnet.

Yes, Mom was a woman who welcomed all and when Christ said, "Welcome the stranger," Mom heeded the call and so have I. Oddly enough getting back to praying the Rosary on a daily basis is a tribute to Mom and Dad. It is part and parcel to the faith they have instilled in us.

MY PARENTS

Walter J. Zalot. Sr.
and Anna Mae Zalot

A YEAR OF GRACE

In loving memory of Walter J. Zalot, Sr.
June 30, 1924-March 17, 2001

As Father's Day approaches and the date that would have been Dad's eighty-third birthday drew near, it is hard not to remember that last year of Dad's life as anything but a year of grace. It was a year of great favor from the Lord for my family and me. It had been a year filled with many special moments.

As I look back and reflect on it, I see God's hand in all that had happened to us. No one can say anything except the fact that the death of Dad on March 17, 2001 ended a successful 53-year marriage in which two people lived for their family and each other! Mom and Dad were married on January 31,

1948.

For many years Dad had been my arms and legs. He took me everywhere, allowing me to be a living witness for God. I am disabled and need others to bathe, shave and dress me. For most of the last two years of Dad's life my brothers and brothers-in-law took over these tasks despite obligations to their own families. Dependency puts a very real strain on family relationships. Dad felt relieved once the help of a permanent caregiver was in place. This addition helped to relieve the strain on the family. I have no doubt this is one of the big reasons why this year, a year of grace was a gift from God for our family.

In October of 2000 the burden from the family was lifted as I got an attendant to help me with the needs of daily living. Now, I don't feel the burden I once felt my disability placed on my family. A burden about my being taken care for was lifted from Dad's shoulders as well as my own. This also allowed Dad and me too to develop our relationship as two adults and not just as parent/child. Dependency on my part of him didn't let that relationship mature until those final months. Out of everything that took place in Dad's last months, I'm most grateful that this began.

This is why I feel a long-term illness like heart disease, which took my father's life, sometimes gave surviving family members an opportunity to adjust to the reality of the person's pending death. I took advantage of the time that was given him to adjust to the reality and pushed to get much needed help for myself. The paperwork and other barriers to get that needed aid frustrated us all. It took nearly nine months to get the help for me, lifting the burden from my family. From February of 1999 until the time I got a full time aid which began on October 1, 2000, I felt the cross of my disability as never before in my life. I felt as though a real burden was lifted off my family.

Likewise, it also afforded Dad an opportunity to get his affairs in order. Dad took advantage of this chance with courage and faith. His illness never stopped Dad from doing what he wanted to do for his family and others in need.

On Friday, March 16, 2001 for example, the night before he died Mom and Dad went to Mass and The Stations of the Cross. As usual, Dad drove. It was to be their last public act of worship. This simple act exemplified how they lived their lives of faith together. This is how they celebrated every Friday of Lent for as long as I could remember. When we were younger, we did this pious act as family. It reminded me, as Bishop Sheen stated so often, "without a cross, there is no resurrection."

On Saturday, March 17, Mom and Dad spent the day together. They shopped as they had done so many Saturdays. Dad had two bowls of spaghetti for dinner, watched a movie until 9-p.m. when dad went into the bathroom and collapsed. He had a heart attack. He was never revived.

The year began with an unusual assignment for me. I was asked by an editor of a Catholic magazine to write a feature on the death of a caregiver from the perspective of the person depending on him. I had no clue as to where to start, so, I decided to read a book on the subject of death and dying. The book I read was *A Gift of Peace*. This classic by Joseph Cardinal Bernardin helped me direct my focus for the article as well as prioritizing my objectives throughout this year of grace.

The book focused on the last three years of the Cardinal's life. Reading this book gave me time to see how I could approach this very difficult task of looking at death from a Christian perspective. It also made me see what is important in life; namely, faith, family and friends.

One of those friends, an Extraordinary minister of the Eucharist, gave Mom, Dad and me a very special gift. We were able to receive Jesus in the Eucharist as family nearly every day since November of 1999. Due to Dad's heart condition, we were unable to receive the Blessed Sacrament together as a family for many years. This friend gave us that chance.

I am grateful God gave Dad this year of grace. In July of 2000 we celebrated the wedding of my youngest brother John. (A year later, in July of 2001, John and his wife Amy had their first child). A month early, in June of 2000, Dad was blessed to see two grandsons graduate from high school. In May of 2002 his oldest granddaughter graduated from the University of Alabama with a Bachelor of Science in Psychology and two other granddaughters graduated from high school in June 2002. It has been a time of favor and grace from the Lord.

Dad also knows his eleventh grandchild was due to

be born in July of 2001. The child was born several weeks early, June 8, 2001. This child's birth was nothing short of miracle. After ten years of marriage, my sister Annie and my brother-in-law Joe had their first child. In October of 2002 they had their second. The number of grandchildren would reach 13. It certainly was a year of grace from the Lord.

Over 200 attended his wake the night before. On that night members of the local Chapter of Knights of Columbus, which Dad belonged to since 1976, stood guard over his body at attention in view of the Blessed Sacrament. It was something I will always remember.

Lastly, the day of Dad's funeral, March 22, 2001 our Blessed Lord gave me a rare privilege. I, the disabled son, whom he covered nightly, pulled the blanket to his shoulders, before his coffin was closed and we celebrated a Mass of Christian burial for this loving husband, father of nine, and now grandfather of 15, uncle, brother and friend to so many. At least on that day, I finally saw our roles reverse. The previous evening, at Dad's viewing; I placed this poem in his casket:

NOW YOU HAVE PERFECT HEARING

Now you have perfect hearing,
And I don't have the words to say,
We had many misunderstandings,
Your disability got in the way.

I thought in attempting to tell you
I wanted to speak in another way,
Might have helped you understand,
But rephrasing things created obstacles every day.

Now that you have perfect hearing,
The small talk that cluttered each day;
Seems so unimportant now,
Both our limitations got in the way.

Dad, despite our distance,
I now know you approved of my life's pathway,
You will help me through my writing,
Make a difference in the life of others everyday!

> With love, your son,
> BILL

Knowing that none of us will need such help, because we'll be free of our imperfections and limitations at our resurrection, gives us much comfort! Also, our hope as Catholics is that we'll all see all our faith filled loved ones at the resurrection on the last day! This truth is the source of great joy; tempering the sadness of our losses on our earthly journey!

A MOTHER'S LOVE

Mass and receiving Jesus is the highlight of my day. During the week I go as often as possible. Before Mass recently I prayed God would show me his presence in a concrete way in the lives of others. I was surprised in the ways God answered that prayer. I saw it in the courage of a woman who cantered for the first time in our church. Her gentle voice added much to the liturgy as did the guitarist. He played beautifully I saw God's presence in the pride of the cantor's family who was present there. I saw it the reverence in which the mass was celebrated. Yet, I saw it most profoundly in the interaction between a mother and her son.

We all know a mother sometimes needs to have the patience of a saint. She needs to understand the temperament of her child. In displaying such control a mother illustrates the compassion of Christ. I saw this at a weekday mass during the season of Lent in 2009.

The four-year-old climbing the pew bumped his chest as the mass neared its end. The only harsh words from that mom who must have been at wits end I heard were, "that's what you get for acting up. Don't do it again!"

But then this mom rubbed the injured part, consoling her sobbing son. I thought to myself "Mom might have done the same." The mass was nearly ended. Those of us gathered were told to "Go in peace…" I believe those of us who encountered this Mom and her kids had a clearer understanding of Christ's compassion than when this Eucharistic Liturgy began. I left that Church thinking about the following:

How many of us have been there with a squirming child? Might we have been that rambunctious child ourselves in our early childhood? Too often we are quick to judge the mom and the child or children, without really knowing their circumstances.

In seeing Moms who bring their children to mass I see a breed of women that wish to pass on the faith by showing compassion and love to their children. Often while seeing these moms I am reminded of my own Mom who was an exemplary example of such a woman. I am the third oldest of nine children. If that doesn't tell one that Mom loved children, then the fact that she babysat countless numbers through the years should. For she never made much money on her efforts due to the fact that our Mom often fed those children who were in her care several meals a day. It seemed Mom's kitchen never closed. I often said, "Mom, you are the best cook ever!" I think I saw "the multiplication of the loaves and fish" take place in our home on countless occasions. Mom certainly knew how to stretch a meal. No matter who dropped by, they were always welcomed to dine with us.

She welcomed cousins and even an uncle who needed a "temporary home." In my uncle's case the situation ended 20 years later with his death. Mom and Dad always welcomed the stranger and there was none stranger than our Uncle Frank. He lived with us from 1956 until his death in 1976. His temporary stay certainly earned our Mom and Dad both brownie points towards their eternal rewards.

Yes, Mom was a woman who welcomed all and when Christ said, "Welcome the stranger," Mom heeded that call taking Christ at his word literally and so have I.

Thank you, Theresa, (I don't know her last name), your example at mass reminded of my own Mother. You are a shining example of a Mother's love!

REMEMBERING THAT PERFECT CHRISTMAS GIFT

There are many memories of past Christmases for each of us. I must admit looking at the many Christmases in my life the Christmas of 1989 stands out as the one that I see with more significance than others before or since. That Christmas, my parents gave me a perfect gift, affirming my vocation as a freelance-writer. The gift was a word processor.

One of the feature stories I'm most proud of is one in which I stretched myself, forcing myself to see the author far beyond my limitations. The feature on Michelangelo's "Pieta'' had an unexpected benefit - completing the task helped me deal with a younger brother's death which occurred back in March of 1992. The day I completed the work a postcard arrived at my home with Michelangelo's "Pieta'' on it. I held the card in my hand for a long time and wept.

In my mind God was saying with that mail from a friend as if by God himself to say, "Great job, my son!" I have kept that postcard to remind me how God affirms us in such ordinary ways. I have also kept the postcard as a reminder to pray for the person who sent the card to me.

Like sacred art, the holy image depicted on that postcard drew my thoughts to Our Blessed Mother holding the lifeless body of her beloved son, Jesus, forever etched in stone. Isn't this image a reminder to mothers who have lost children that Mary understands? It shows me she can be united with us in our sufferings.

That one image tells us neither she nor Jesus were spared from the human condition of suffering. These thoughts are consoling. The day I sold the story I ordered a replica of the masterpiece for Mom and wept. These days I hope the images depicted in the statue give Mom some consolation. I know when I view this marbled masterpiece it comforts me.

Words are the tools of my craft. I am a professional writer. Although my mom and dad had always found it difficult to affirm my talents as a writer with words of encouragement, I know they believed in me, for in 1989, they affirmed my vocation. That year, Mom and Dad gave me a perfect gift for Christmas. That gift for years helped me develop my craft.

That treasured gift that spoke volumes to me their

son with a physical disability; spastic cerebral palsy, was a word processor!

Thank you, Mom and Dad! That gift empowered me like few had in my life. I will always love you, merry Christmas to one and all and best wishes for the coming year!

AN ANGEL FOR CHRISTMAS

An Angel of the Lord, Gabriel, Appeared to Tell Mary of Jesus' Virgin Birth

We all need angels — people who have a real impact on our lives at critical moments. As I am a person with a disability spastic cerebral palsy, I have seen many such individuals, men and women sent by God, come in and out my life. This is the story of one such angel who came into my life six years ago this December. I will call him Michael to protect his privacy.

Until February of 2000, my father had taken care of my daily needs. He was 30 years my senior. He bathed me, dressed me and helped me with other bathroom needs, from shaving to cleaning my bottom.

From February through October of 2000, my brothers and brothers-in-law had taken over those responsibilities while I was on the waiting list to get an attendant. Despite obligations to their own jobs and families, these caring individuals shared the responsibilities of taking care of me.

From February to October of 2000, I waited for papers to be processed. In August, the agency that began the process dropped me, suddenly, like a hot potato. My family and I had to fill out the same paperwork for the new government agency that took over my case. Cheryl, my caseworker at the time for that new agency, which still oversees my care, calmly told me, "William, the process will take about six months."

"Bull****!" was my response. I told her of my family's struggle over the previous eight months. The ordeal had put enormous strain on our relationships. I had enough of being a pawn, just another number. I was angry. My health and my dad's fragile health were at risk. I wasn't going to be pushed around anymore. These days another woman oversees my case.

For me personally, constipation became more of a problem than usual. I knew someone would help me each day, but I never knew the time.

As a result I had a difficult time regulating myself. During this period of transition I had several accidents, messing my pants. This time in my life, I felt the cross of my dependency a greater burden than ever before. I wasn't a happy person.

I feared the possibility of being sent to a nursing facility. I knew that, for my own health, the situation had to change. This young caseworker had my future in her hands. She was a rookie. Realizing that I was one of her first cases frightened me.

I came out fighting just as I had fought for everything in my life, so, why should this be different? I felt as never before, my personal future was on the line. If I wasn't willing to fight, who would take my cause?

My tough talk sprang Cheryl into action. I became her personal crusade. She contacted several agencies and the process was expedited. Within weeks, her agency subcontracted someone through a private agency. By mid-October I had a personal care-giver named Robin. Over the next four or five weeks that she was with me I got comfortable.

During days when the weather was good, Robin took me for long walks around the neighborhood. This single mom told me how working with me made it possible to get the Christmas gifts she wanted for her daughter. This talk gave me a sense of security. After the first week, I was able to regulate myself on Robin's schedule. Her first day on the job, just before getting me in the tub, I needed to use the toilet.

The moment she sat on the edge of tub, placed me across her knees and she thoroughly wiped my backside, I sensed things would be all right. Though I was 46, bent over across young woman's lap, I felt like a child about to be spanked. One of my biggest fears was conquered that day; having an employee that wipes my bottom instead of a family member! Not since my days at college was that the case. And the student worker bathing or taking care of my toilet needs was never a woman.

Looking back, I was glad God let me figuratively get back on the horse during Robin's first day. I know now, this made me too at ease. I was not on my guard enough to see trouble ahead. But there came another day, early in November. I invited Robin to the mall, to help me with some Christmas shopping. We used Paratransit, the region's public transportation for physically disabled people. Among the services Paratransit provides are vans with wheelchair lifts.

Once our shopping was done, we waited over two hours for our expected pick-up to go home. Both of us were more than a little angry. She swore she couldn't do it again.

Robin remained my attendant for several more weeks. In late October the agency she worked for announced it was closing its Philadelphia branch, and I decided to hire this young woman under another agency.

Under the agency's consumer option she agreed and I thought we were set. I was wrong. Days before Thanksgiving, Robin left my home, never to be seen again. A door had closed; I waited for a window to be opened.

It would take a few weeks to replace this young woman. However, my caseworker took the fast lane to replace her. The agency which has overseen my personal care placed an ad in our local newspaper the first week of December, when it was clear Robin wasn't returning.

The ad ran for a week. The first day it appeared in the local newspaper, I found the person to do the job. I interviewed him that very day, Dec. 8, the feast of the Immaculate Conception. I know he was a gift from Mary, the Mother of God. He began to work with me on that Monday, Dec. 11. His name was Michael. Although he arrived early, I will always refer to him as my Christmas angel.

Over the past few years, I have come to realize like all of us who are angels of mercy for others, Michael, my Christmas angel has his faults; like all human beings of good will, he wears a crooked halo.

I am glad Dad lived to see this giant, gentle man, who cares for my needs. Dad died a little more than three months after Michael's arrival. My Dad passed away in March of 2001. I feel my Dad was finally at peace knowing I would be cared for. My Dad succumbed to congestive heart failure on March 17, 2001. There was a Mass of Christian burial five days later on March 22, 2001. At his wake the night before, I, the disabled son, had the privilege to cover my Father before his casket was closed for last time. That is a memory I will always treasure!

I have to laugh, I am often informed, without wanting to know, how much it costs Michael to get to my home. Like the Church or a critical parent, the information he tells me brings on feelings of guilt. This feeling of guilt put me in the position that has often made me feel obligated to be his personal loan officer.

Since he doesn't drive, like me, we are both dependant on public transportation. And, more often than not, our thoughts are less than Christian toward its overall operation.

Lastly, my general reaction to his requests for loans as well as my response to his struggles with public transportation is proof positive that it's obvious for the both of us that heaven can wait!

TINY TIM, THE APOSTLE

Dickens' Classic Teaches Us
Another Way to Evangelize

Ever since the South Eastern Pennsylvania Transportation Authority (SEPTA) has been providing transportation for the disabled, I have been able to go Christmas shopping for family and friends. I've done most of my shopping at a bookstore. How many times have the gifts I present to my nieces and nephews come from this bookstore? And I start my shopping early. I often start as soon as August.

My friends think I'm nuts. But it's the only way I can even think about buying something for all the people on my list. Even this I can only accomplish, from my wheelchair, with a little help from my friends. I finish much of my shopping before

Thanksgiving because I hate fighting crowds. Besides, with shopping completed, Advent can be a time for spiritual reflection — which now includes my annual reading of "A Christmas Carol." The book's author, Charles Dickens was born February 7, 1812 at No. 1 Mile End Terrace, Landport, and Portsmouth. He died in 1870.

In the 1991-92, school year I had a CCD student whose birthday was on Christmas Day. I sympathized with her because her great day was overshadowed by a greater day. So, on the last day of class before Christmas vacation, I presented her with the Dickens' classic. But I myself hadn't yet read it, so I borrowed the book from the library.

I fell in love with the story because it is a story of conversion, of one man's journey to understand the plight of the poor. Ghosts of Christmases Past, Present and Future all do their part to change his heart. He sees, too, his own mortality, and this changes him. We readers are invited to look at our own mortality and be changed.

Seeing the death of Tiny Tim Cratchet may have been the turning point in Scrooge's change of heart. This is clearer in the book than in any movie version. Through the Ghost of Christmas Present, Ebenezer saw the impoverished Cratchet family eat their Christmas meal with joy and grateful hearts, in their prayers thanking even old Ebenezer for the feast that lay before them. It was during that visit that Scrooge overheard this conversation:

Mrs. Cratchet asks, "And how was little Tim?" Bob

Cratchet responded, "As good as gold. And better. Somehow he gets thoughtful, sitting by himself so much. The lad sees his disability as a gift." The peace and joy that radiated from his acceptance of his limitations made others feel at ease around him. People wanted to reach out and help others like Tiny Tim. This included Scrooge, who began that very Christmas by providing the Cratchet family with turkey for their Christmas dinner. Scrooge also would provide funds for Tim's treatment. Ebenezer could see his wealth making a difference in someone's life, while helping him to grow spiritually.

Dickens' book has not lost its power since it first was published in October of 1843. The 160 years since it was first published certainly illustrates to all of us that this tale is a classic. The author in this Christmas classic spoke from the depth of his childhood poverty and has given us a Christmas treasure for the ages. If you haven't read it before, make it your Advent gift to yourself this year.

"I have endeavored in this Ghostly little book," Dickens wrote, "to raise the Ghost of an idea, which shall not put my readers out of humor with themselves, with each other, with the season, or with me. May it haunt their houses pleasantly, and no one wish to lay it down."

THE CHRISTMAS CHARIOT

Marge Martin is a widow in her mid-fifties. She is a beautiful princess in the eyes of this admirer and a witch in the mind of some others in our small community. Few people see what I see. In realty, she probably is somewhere in between. Like all of us, this woman has flaws and is a sinner. Nevertheless, this is a woman I have come to love and I would give her the world if I could.

The Power of Forgiveness

I've known Marge for nearly six years and one of the greatest lessons I've learned from her is the power of forgiveness; both forgiving oneself and being forgiven by the one we hurt. We are called to live the challenge of "The Lord's Prayer." Still, in the incident I am about to refer to without mentioning the details, if I were not forgiven, I don't think I could have forgiven myself.

In all that time I have come to realize she is a strong willed woman who has been hurt by life's circumstances many times. This fact most certainly has contributed to people's misperception that she lacks an ability to have trust in nearly anyone or anything. I don't see that at all. For I know one of her greatest attributes is her ability to forgive when one is truly repentant and willing to change. I found this out first-hand; days after I made a commitment to purchase a wheelchair for her we had a huge fallout. Devastated, I thought I lost her friendship. Nonetheless, I was going to keep the promise I made back in July.

My heart was broken and I was forced to examine my actions. Making a promise to God, Marge and myself to change I knew I must repent – saving a friendship and perhaps my life as I knew it.

That day, we became peers; I listened and heard her words as never before. In her ability to forgive me, I saw Christ. Due to misperceptions and for her to keep her own sanity she has placed a protective shell like a turtle between herself and those of us around her. I wished to stay in that inner-circle. I wanted our relationship to grow.

For me, this protective mode was best illustrated when she saw to it that I got breakfast, lunch and supper for two weeks while my attendant was on vacation early in the fall of 2009. Marge has been there for me. In fact, we have been there for each other. We have helped each other to grow. Within our friendship we have found shelter that has made us feel safe. I can't or won't speak for others in her inner-circle, but only about myself and how I feel.

Decades ago this woman was a teacher. Today, she still uses these same skills to impact the lives of those around her. I am one who has benefited from her wealth of knowledge. In an earlier part of my life I taught also. This common factor has allowed us to understand each other better. This remarkable woman also has a number of disabilities that forces her to use a wheelchair, though I have used my mobility vehicle longer than her. We are learning from each other, which for me brings back memories of other close relationships.

Through her I have drawn on fond memories of those days. Like a good wine, those reflections get better with age. Like the angel in "its A Wonderful Life," she reminds me time and again of the many lives I have touched.

Like most of the relationships in my life, I thought this one was fragile. Therefore, I wanted to put some safeguards in place and so I did. These measures have protected us as a cocoon protects a caterpillar. They include the following in no particular order:

1. I must take a hand urinal where ever I go to minimize the help I need from her.

2. I can't drink apple cider for lunch (must drink it later in the day).

3. Whenever possible wear shorts.

4. Know if bathrooms are wheelchair accessible.

5. Whenever possible avoid being lifted into or out of a car, because I do not feel comfortable with the process. I do not want anyone getting hurt including myself.

6. Respect each other's space.

7. Know the difference between a want and a need.

8. Be willing to take risks and be flexible.

9. Step out in faith to fill a need or be present for one another.

10. Seek forgiveness when you've wronged the other and be willing to forgive.

By the items one, two and three on the list one can surmise that this young lover (Marge corrected me, "this middle-age man") has bathroom issues. Timing is everything, why let the truth get in the way of a good story?

It was mid-summer 2009 when Margie brought back memories of a Christmas in my distant past when she asked me "What Christmas gift had the most impact on your life?" I kissed her cheek and answered without hesitation "the word processor my parents gave me."

What more did I have to say. In my eyes that word processor affirmed that my parents believed I had the talent to tell a good story. Within months of getting that gift my first feature was sold. Each sale affirmed my folks' belief in me.

From past experience though, I know a woman doesn't just ask a question without having something in mind. I wondered just what was on her mind. Soon

I found out what she needed and the Holy Spirit showed me how I could help get it for her. She never asked for my help, but I provided it.

The two of us went to a baseball game; a Businessperson's Special, I saw the tilt prevention bars fall off. A kind gentleman snapped them back on. These bars prevent a wheelchair from flipping over while going up or down a curb. This was one of several times I saw one of the bars come off. I promised her that day, "Marge, I will get the wheelchair for you." In truth, she never asked me.

I thought to myself, "How?" All I knew is I could not let her down. I was shaking. I made a promise. God would have to help me keep it. God surprised me with the answer. "You already have the means."

Of course I did, but I wondered what would family say? Only time revealed that answer. Regardless of what they thought I was going to get my princess a Chariot for Christmas. And hoped that this gift had half the impact the word processor had on my life. I knew in my heart that it would truly make a difference!

Thanks to a sibling's suggestion, the seed had been planted nearly a year before, my Christmas club account would be the answer! I believed I could make it happen for nothing is impossible with God.

I found a way, sending her a check each month. By December there was an air of anticipation. I felt as happy as Scrooge must of felt after his transformation; as joyful as s child awaiting the arrival of his first pet.

Christmas-eve of 2009 arrived. We attended mid-night Mass, something I hadn't done this since I was a young boy. The Liturgy was wonderful. I heard the Gospel with expectant faith. The Christmas story seemed fresh. I knew it was in part because of who was with me.

Mass ended at 1:40 on Christmas morning and we had an early breakfast at an all night diner. Served and finished by 3:00 am we went home.

Upon arriving home I handed Margie a pair of scissors to cut the ribbon around the chair's arms. Nervously, she began to cut the ribbon. Tears welled up in both of our eyes.

Tired, we kissed each other a good night and wished each other a Merry Christmas. I then went to my own apartment thanking God for all He had done in our lives. It was a wonderful day. For I knew in my heart, as the couple in O. Henry's "Gift of the Magi," we had given all we had.

When I think back to the Christmas of 2009, I don't think of gifts I didn't give, or my travel plans delayed by weather—rather, I think of one Christmas gift I did and how it has impacted one life that has touched so many others. I also think of the friendship God's grace saved and for that, I am most grateful.

Since that time Margie has volunteered as an advocate, is a strong voice for the pro-life movement and runs several bible studies. The Christmas Chariot I bought her has become living Wheels for Christ as she travels sharing the good news.

May the Holy Spirit who inspired me the

Christmas of 2009 to step out in faith and change
someone's life inspire all who read this story to do the
same!

THE CHRISTMAS BOX

Imagine for a moment, that a lifetime of Christmas memories would be stored like decorations in a Christmas box. This storage chest of treasures may include letters, snapshots, home movies and more. As you read one of my most treasured Christmas memories, you may think back to one of your own.

It was a Christmas nearly half a century ago. The memory I'll reflect on took place in 1964. I pick it out from my Christmas box of memories; and wish to share with you. It is about a toy car I had but a few hours before it was broken.

The memory is associated with a Matchbox car with one missing wheel. That tiny car's tire was lost in the snow on Christmas Day. My cousin Bobby broke it as he grabbed it from my hands that afternoon when he visited. The automobile model was a Mustang. The pale blue car was a perfect addition to my growing collection. I was ten as was he. He profusely asked for my forgiveness and I gave it to him though I was deeply hurt.

That Christmas was the first time I realized forgiveness had nothing to do with feelings. Rather, forgiveness is a conscious act. Although I verbally accepted his apology, my heart lagged behind. I am not a saint.

Halfway through that Christmas Day, my heart went along with my spoken acceptance to forgive him shortly after the incident. Almost immediately, the knot in my stomach eased.

It was one of the first times in my life I saw in a personal way how the decision to forgive can affect ones health. This is regardless of whether the forgiveness is accepted or not by the person to whom it is intended.

It is fitting I learned this lesson on Christmas when we celebrate Christ's birth. This realization made the Christmas I was ten, a very special Christmas. It remains a golden nugget in my Christmas box of memories. The power of that forgiveness has allowed the two of us to remain lifetime friends.

Merry Christmas and I wish you His Peace in the coming year!

A CHRISTMAS MEMORY,
A PARISH ANNIVERSARY
& FEELING WELCOMED

C an the physical design of a church as well as the attitude of its pastor and his associate pastors make the physically-challenged person feel welcomed or unwelcomed in a parish community? As a Catholic, who happens to be disabled, I have pondered this question many times over the years. However, it wasn't until I experienced a moment of grace, Christmas Eve 1997, that I could answer that question with a resounding, "Yes!"

A Night I Went to the Mountaintop

On that holy night, Christmas Eve 1997, I had a "Mountaintop Experience" at Our Lady of Sorrows, in Trenton, New Jersey. My niece Rebecca and nephew Michael were altar servers. Their Mom and Dad, my brother-in-law Mike, and my sister his wife were also part of the service. Mike was a lector that evening and my sister Rosemary was an Extraordinary Minister of the Eucharist. We were blessed that special night as my parents, and my brother John and I celebrated our Catholic faith together at that 5:30 PM Christmas Eve Vigil Mass.

The priest, Father Pat, an associate pastor, gave a powerful homily. Part of the talk was on Dorothy Day and the dignity of each human being. In that sermon, one the stories he used, was about the time Day gave a woman a diamond ring in her soup kitchen. The story touched me deeply. Still, the highlight of the Liturgy for me, was receiving Jesus, in the Blessed Sacrament from my sister Rosemary.

I felt totally accepted, hugged by God. That evening, when I got home, overwhelmed by the experience, I just described, I wept, wept for joy. The grounds of the church and rectory were clearly posted with several marked signs, each one inscribed with the international symbol of the disabled.

Each one, like the trumpets which must have accompanied Gabriel, as he announced the Good News, told me, and all disabled people, "You are welcomed here!"

As a disabled person, the physical layout of a church, as well as the attitude of a church's pastor, associate pastors and community at large can all play a role in allowing a person with a disability to feel welcomed. Complete access made me feel welcomed that Christmas Eve.

Today, I feel welcomed and at home in most Catholic Churches. For many reasons, this wasn't always the case. Still, steps, if I think about it, on at least a subconscious level, make me wonder, "Am I really welcomed here?"

What Has Gotten Me to Think About These Things?

I wish I could say it was a nudge from an enlightened editor, but, in fact, I found a personal journal reflection on the subject as St. Michael the Archangel Church, Levittown, PA, was about to celebrate its 45th anniversary in January of 1998. My parents were founding members of the parish and I have been a lifetime member of the parish community. Until I was 11 or 12, I recall Mass being celebrated in the school gym. Prior to the school's completion, founding families celebrated Mass and the Sacraments at the town's firehouse until the parish school was completed.

I don't recall those early days. The Parish, Levittown's first Catholic Community, was established January 21, 1953 and I was born June 27, 1954, nearly a year and a half after Saint Mike's was founded. I recall with fondness, the intimacy of celebrating Mass and the Sacraments in my early childhood years. For me, that closeness was gone when I was 11 or 12.

Remembering the Completion of
Our Million-Dollar Parish "Home"

I don't often think about it. Because when I do, it evokes anger and bitterness towards the Parish. Or more accurately toward those who made the decisions in designing this Church. In truth, I felt, it was a monument to our founding Pastor Monsignor Joseph Collins. The building was completed in January of 1966.

Rightly or wrongly, I blamed the founding pastor; a priest from the old-school of method of thinking. It seemed as if he called the shots: as stated this building and its design was a monument to him alone. He would fit in quite nicely with today's evangelist like Robert Schuller and his Crystal Cathedral. Without saying a word, the design of Saint Mike's told me I was not welcomed. Monsignor Collins often told my family, "There is no need to bring him here!" bringing home the point.

Thankfully, my parents didn't take his advice. They brought me to Mass each week. Still, his words angered me. Each time I saw the two flights of steps in front of the Church the steps told me "it was not important for me to be there." They stung like my disability stung my Dad anew each time he came home from work. Church was where I felt the least accepted of anywhere I went. At age 12, I certainly didn't know of St. Lawrence who thought the lame, blind, poor and widowed of the church were the true treasures for which he died.

Looking back at our founding Pastor's actions I

realize the saint of the early Church (mentioned in the previous paragraph) was not a role-model for him. For St. Lawrence, a Deacon who died a martyr's death in 258 AD, has since become a hero of mine. Like Mother Teresa, his example has shown me the worth and dignity of each person. Our founding pastor's attitude made me more bound and determined to be there. This was despite my safety or the safety of others who may have been handling me up those steps. In my child's mind, I only saw a vengeful God who would condemn me to Hell, if I missed Mass. I didn't know God as a God of mercy. Missing Mass on Sunday or holy days intentionally is a mortal sin, however, if weather or illness prevents one from attending Mass one must recall the "just God" is indeed also a God of Mercy.

In my youth, I acted foolishly. My perception of God had to change. I had the perception rightly or wrongly that the design of the church was made with little consideration for those of us with disabilities. Over the years, I have come to realize the design of the Church was in part a reflection of the times, rather than his sole judgment.

With this understanding I am able to forgive the founding pastor. In the same light, I am able to forgive myself for risking my father's health or the health of others in all kinds of weather to get to Mass in fear of a vengeful God. I gave little consideration to the real risk to others in handling me. It took years, of personal growth and maturity to come to this realization.

Through a friend I have come to know in a very personal way the depth of God's mercy. In truth, concern for this individual has made me more aware of the real risk for her. Seeing her slip down the church's ramp partially awoke me to the real risk in inclement weather. That incident was like a slap in the face for me. If, this woman would have gotten hurt, I would have had a hard time forgiving myself. In a real sense, this episode contributed a great deal to my maturity as a Christian.

Years before (August 1979-May 1982) a change in my view from an isolationist to an activist in the Church slowly took root. The personal growth had its seeds at West Chester State College's Newman Center. It was there I began to realize I could no longer be just an "Obligated" or "Sunday Catholic." I had to live my faith every day. Involvement in the Newman Center sparked life into my faith. By meeting Christ daily in the Eucharist, I began to come to know a loving, merciful God, not a vengeful God, not the God I perceived as a child.

The transformation continued when I got home. A former Army Chaplain had become St. Mike's fourth pastor. He played a major role in making me feel like a vital part of the parish community.

Coupled with my faith that grew at the Newman Center, Father Speitel was the right individual for the time. His spirit softened my heart towards the parish and had given me a desire for service to him and the community.

A Challenge That Opened Doors

I saw him as a gentle spirit. Although he had a gruff exterior, this former Army Chaplain had a "shepherd's heart." It showed me how he was a motivator and I saw personally how this shepherd of our parish community was such a hard man to refuse.

How I found this out first hand is quite a story. In retelling it, I hope I capture the extent of the impact it had on me. He wanted me to write a series of articles on the role of the disabled in the church today for our parish bulletin.

I didn't think twice about his offer. Though, I can't imagine either of us could have dreamt the doors that were opened as a result of my acceptance of his off-the-cuff challenge. On second thought, perhaps, Father Speitel did, but, I know, I didn't.

Due to my increased involvement, I no longer felt detached from the parish. St. Michael the Archangel Church had truly become my spiritual home. His persuasiveness allowed me to be convinced to dive into the heart of parish life.

Prior to doing the series, I felt more at home or welcomed at neighboring parishes due in part to accessibility. I had even begun to lector at one of those churches. Several of those parishes were within a short driving distance. A blessing resulting from this time in my life is that I had friends from all those parish communities. A downside to it in recent years has been that I have been to funeral Masses in each of those parishes due to the friendships and relationships which have developed.

Shortly after the series was completed, a man who desired to convert to Catholicism approached our Pastor, saying. "I want to become Catholic, if that young man who wrote the series on the role of the disabled in the Church today could sponsor me."

I got a telephone call from our Pastor that same day. He shared the above story with me as the man and his wife were still in his office. He ended the conversation with, "I want to bring this man into the Church Friday. Bill, can you do it?"

I paused before responding, "I am not sure I can get a ride."

"The Candidate and his wife have agreed to pick you up," was his prepared response. He then said, "They're in my office now!"

I asked, "What Mass?"

I figure it was his military humor kicking in when he declared, "6:30 A.M."

I responded, "If it's the eight, you have a deal."

He agreed and that Friday the man converted. His wife and I were witnesses. I was given a watch to mark the occasion. Though the watch is but a memory of that day in 1992, my involvement has been evolving.

Today I lector, I am also a member of Knights of Columbus with the rank of Third Degree, and am our parish's representative for the Archdiocese of Philadelphia's Office for Persons with Disabilities.

Over the years, I have discovered until one offered their gifts or talents to their parish or community, their eyes won't be open to how God is working in the life of others and therefore making a difference.

Your talents, your gifts like those shared by my brother-in-law, sister, niece and nephew may help someone have a mountaintop experience like I did those many Christmases ago.

A Cry for Help

"Father, if it be Your will take this Cup from me..."

These words were spoken by Christ the night before He died for us. Deserted by his companions, Christ must have felt very much alone as he prayed to his Father. Yet, we read as the prayer continues "nevertheless, Thy will be done, not mine!"

This is a prayer of surrender. It is the type of prayer we need to pray in difficult circumstances. Mary prayed that type of prayer at the Annunciation "Let it be done to me, according to Thy Word," Mary had no idea what that "Yes" meant. Yet, she certainly walked in faith. It was indeed a prayer of surrender and acceptance.

Life's circumstances can help us reach out to others in similar situations. And those less fortunate than ourselves. We like Mary may not understand what changes such a prayer may bring to our lives. The challenges could bring us closer to Jesus as he walks though our lives with us. The late Bishop Sheen often stated, "Without a cross there is no Resurrection," We will find this to be true as we walk through the challenges of our daily lives.

The Cup or Cross we ask to be taken away may be

the very source of our salvation or someone else's. If we can accept the splinters of our visible or invisible crosses of our lives imagine who we may lead to Christ. Reflecting on what Christ suffered beginning in that Garden of love we can gain strength to accept our Crosses in life.

A cry for help may not take our crosses away, but it may bring into our lives the help we need to carry them. As described in the Fifth Station Simon reluctantly at first helps Christ carry His cross. An appropriate prayer to say at the end of this Station could be:

Oh Jesus, so many times I find myself afraid to help You carry the cross, to follow You in all things, to do your will at each moment. Our Holy Father Saint Dominic was the Preacher of Truth, who echoed Your promise that truth will set us free. Help me to know the truth about myself. Give me the grace to put effort in forming habits of virtue, and inspire me to go out of myself in service to You and to others.

How many Simons have been in your life, reluctant or not? I can't count those that have been in mine. They have been men and women who have helped me carry the burdens of my state in life time and again.

As we draw closer to the Holy Week of Christ's Passion and Death send prayers of intercession for those who have lifted you in your time of need. Give thanks for them being there.

As I see it, God may not "Take our Cup Away" but I pray He will give us the strength and faith to bear it!

May the sorrow of Good Friday bring us to the hope of the Resurrection that is the real joy of Easter!

A WAY TO SEE LIFE

Sometimes words hit us square in the face and remind us how we have been blessed. Such was the case for me the other day. As I knocked on the door of a neighbor I read the quote tacked to her front door. The words made me realize just how blessed I am. The quote attributed to Helen Keller inspired me to get off my pity-pot. The words are simple, yet can force any of us to truly count our blessings. We can profess these words as a prayer, making them our own: "With all I have been given, I have no time to ponder that which has been denied." What a prayer of thanksgiving! It is an awesome way to view life!

Helen Keller and I share the same birthday. Well, not exactly. She was born on June 27, 1880. For the record, I was born on that date in 1954. Unlike me,

Helen Keller was born perfectly normal. A mysterious illness beset her at 19 months, changing her life and the life of her family.

Keller became the first deaf and blind individual to earn a Bachelor of Arts degree from Radcliff. As a young man, inspired by her success, Helen's example gave me a reason to dream. Angry at the world, like Helen, I took my feelings out on those around me. From an early age, again like Keller, I wrote to channel my emotions.

Like many, I was first introduced to the triumphs and struggles of this hero through the Academy Award winning motion picture from 1962; "Miracle Worker."

In a darkened theater, when I saw Patty Duke as Helen utter her first word, "water," I cried and cheered. The film, tells the story of the first few years in which Helen worked with Anne Sullivan. Ann Bancroft, who portrayed Anne Sullivan, won an Academy Award for that 1962 performance as Helen's lifelong friend and teacher. The film still moves me all these years later.

Anne and Helen traveled the world, as lecturers, teachers and writers; imagine how many lives they touched! Helen died in 1959 at the age of 78.

It is my hope this reflection gives all who read it a new way to see life, regardless of their state in life! I know the words tacked to my neighbor's door had an impact on me.

THEY CARRY CHRIST

Remembering a Special Time of Grace

While I was in college, I got into the habit of attending Mass and receiving Our Blessed Lord in the Eucharist nearly every day. Jesus gives us "real food and real drink" at every Mass (see John 6:54). It is food for my journey.

Knowing I would participate in a late-afternoon or early-evening Mass at West Chester's Newman Center got me through my days. College isn't easy for anyone; nor was it easy for me. With my disability, spastic cerebral palsy, I must use a wheelchair to get around.

In 1982 I graduated. I was a changed man; my faith was alive. I was no longer just an obligated Catholic. I sought a community of believers to replace the Newman Center Community I'd left behind upon graduation from college.

At that time, over two decades ago, a local parish offered a 7 p.m. Mass daily. So I found ways to drag someone to take me two or three times a week. The "Angels of Mercy," as I dubbed them, were old and young alike. Our common denominator was our love for the Eucharist. For more than 10 years, Our Lord kept this network together. Those years were a time of special grace.

But age, life changes and people moving on ebbed away the network. Then the parish eliminated its 7 p.m. Mass, and so went my opportunities for daily Communion.

Still, I was not a typical shut-in. My activities in the parish make me a visible and active member of our Church. Yet it's difficult for me to get to a morning Mass.

For several years, I could get to Mass only on Sundays and holy days. Yet I longed for another chance to receive Jesus more frequently.

As the Jubilee Year 2000 drew near, God answered my prayer. A friend from a neighboring parish — one of my former Angels of Mercy — became an extraordinary minister of the Eucharist.

Extraordinary ministers of Holy Communion are lay people appointed by the bishop or pastor to distribute the sacrament when there are not enough ordained ministers to do so. They bring Jesus to those in need, by visiting homes, hospitals or nursing homes, often seeing the same people week after week. Their visits touch the most vulnerable members of the Body of Christ; the elderly, those with disabilities and those who are lonely and forgotten experience compassion in the selfless acts of the people chosen to serve in this ministry.

Thus my friend Joe Sheenan began to bring Jesus to my parents and me, several days a week from mid-December 1999 until Dad's death in March of 2001. This man's efforts made the time a period of grace for the three of us. This humble act allowed Mom, Dad and me to celebrate our faith as a family. This is something we were unable to do for years as a family due my Dad's health. Dad couldn't lift me into his car anymore.

Joe Sheenan's ministry touched our lives on several levels: spiritually, of course, but it has also changed my social life. His visits break the routine of just having family around. We interrupt the television's blaring and begin our prayer with the Sign of the Cross and the plea for God's mercy. We read one of several passages from John's Gospel or one of his letters, and we pray the Our Father together. We state our unworthiness to receive Jesus and pray for His healing for each of us. Then we received Him.

When you see a Eucharistic minister at Mass, remember you are only seeing a fraction of how they serve your parish. To people like me and my family, they bring Jesus daily, and present Him, Body, Blood, Soul and Divinity in the Eucharist.

A woman from a parish in Philadelphia who has

served as a Eucharistic minister for more than 10 years once told me:

"If the visible tip of an iceberg is only 10 percent of its total, then distributing the Holy Eucharist at Mass is only 10 percent of this ministry's total; the other 90 percent remains invisible." But this ministry will not be forgotten by those touched by it.

As what would have been Dad's 84TH birthday, June 30th 2008 approaches, I remembered this time of grace. A time when Christ, put in a mini-Tabernacle of sorts, a pyx, which can be safely hidden in a pants, shirt or jacket pocket was brought to us. Each time this happened my eyes lit up, reflecting the joy in my heart! I know it happens to so many others too.

Therefore, remember in your prayers the Eucharistic minister, for in their pockets, they carry Christ!

PUPPET FOR THE LORD

There is an appointed time for everything...
Ecclesiastes 3:1-8

As I start this brief column, I just finished watching Walt Disney's "Pinocchio." This motion-picture classic, first released in 1940, has become one of my favorite movies of all time. Its simple message of honesty as well as good's triumph over evil is timeless.

However, the fact that this feature-length animated classic reminds us all that temptation is ever present around us, is not lost in the story's telling. In fact, it is a part of the story's charm. It draws viewers through this movie's simple message to watch the film again and again. Each time I watch it, I am spellbound.

The film reminds all of us that we all have free will, temptations are all around us, and this timeless masterpiece helps young and old alike to realize that there are consequences to the choices we make. This truth is part of the fabric of the storyline which creates the film's magic.

As a child I often felt like a puppet controlled by the whims of others and even today there are times I sense others have control of what I can and can't do. I therefore identified with Pinocchio, a puppet, Geppetto the woodcarver's creation.

There were also people in my life that were pulling me in various directions. Even though many of those individuals in his life were attempting to help him, Pinocchio rebelled as I did. He was no one's puppet and neither was I. No one was going to pull his strings, nor were they going to pull mine.

Like me, he didn't want to see the bigger picture. Like him, I was in denial of my limitations and dependency on others. Rather, I knew the truth and closed myself off to life's reality.

In the story, the woodcarver, loving crafted Pinocchio out of wood. In a similar fashion, but with a lot more detail, our heavenly Father has lovingly crafted each one of us.

My dependency on others made me feel like a puppet too. Born with spastic cerebral palsy, as a child, I wanted no one's help. I was angry at God. Like Pinocchio, I felt I was a living puppet, feeling powerless, I felt that everyone was pulling my strings. But, I now know, the people who have come into my life as a result of my disability are blessings from God.

Yes, today as an adult, I realize my dependency on others is part of my mission in life. Glory be to God, these days, I am a puppet for the Lord! I know there is an appointed time for everything under heaven Ecclesiastes 3:1-8. At this time I am called to be God's puppet! My dependency on others helps them and me work out our salvation. Accepting of my status in life makes me a puppet for God the Father is my puppeteer.

These themes which run throughout the movie have values that transcend the generations. This is why I love this film! This is why this movie is a classic.

I also liked the fact the puppet, the dependent and one who is weak, becomes the film's hero. The movie reminds us of a time that Hollywood wasn't amoral as many think it is today.

I also like the fact that a wee small voice, Pinocchio's conscience was represented by a cricket. Like anyone's conscience, this small voice could be squished or ignored by the person to whom it was directed. How often have we done this in our own lives?

For me, the biblical story of Jonah being trapped in the belly of a whale isn't lost. It reminds us that Jonah in the belly of a whale is comparable to Christ's own burial when he lay in a tomb for three days before his resurrection.

Accepting one's role in this life can make an

individual realize one of this movie's taglines can become a reality. I am living proof of that; as a freelance writer, I know a lifelong desire of mine has happened for me: "Dreams can come true!"

A CONVERSION STORY

The Lent and Easter Seasons are swiftly approaching. This time of year makes me think about my own spiritual journey, my conversion from being a "Sunday Catholic" to one who tries to live his faith daily. It is my hope in telling readers the details of my story that they can meet the risen Christ in a more powerful way this Easter. So here goes.

When I arrived at West Chester State College in fall of 1979, I was at best an "obligated Catholic." I showed up for Mass on the obligatory Sunday or holy days of obligation the Church insisted I must, nevertheless, I was angry and I went to Mass out of fear rather than respect or a true desire to be there.

West Chester afforded me the chance to go to daily Mass, when I began do so, the situation gradually changed. Though at first I must admit my motives were far from spiritual. Like many young men in their 20's, I was attracted to a fellow student who went to Mass every day at the college's Newman Center. To make a long story short, I never captured her heart, but Jesus won in! Yes, in my pursuit to win her, Jesus captured me.

As I eased into the routine of Mass — the cycle of feasts and seasons, colors and readings — I began to realize how scripturally-based the Eucharistic Liturgy is.

Yet I was still immature in the faith, and I still held on to my anger. It would take sometime before I understood how much Christ would want me to give Him. And I know if it were not for a chain of events that occurred in the spring of 1981, I may never have surrendered myself to others to the depth God wanted me.

As a person with a physical disability, spastic cerebral palsy, I have always found it relatively easy to tell people of my physical needs. I've used a wheelchair for mobility all my life. Nevertheless, in my 20's I had difficulty speaking to anyone about my emotional needs. In fact, this holding back nearly destroyed me. The story I am about to share, took place in that period of my life:

It was the spring of my junior year. In fact, it was Holy Week. I was doing my field placement at Eagleville Rehabilitation Center. My office mate was one of the program's success stories. A recovered-addict he was now helping others. I looked up to him. On Tuesday, I learned he had fallen back into drug use and was fired. I was angry at that director of the Rehab Center. I was angry at my supervisor.

The next day, Spy Wednesday, I went home for Easter break, hoping to talk with my family about what happened. But other events crowded out my concerns that weekend. I learned that a childhood friend of mine had been sent away to a home for the disabled. I learned, moreover, that this had happened in September! Although I was in touch with my family several times every week, no one had told me. While I was complaining about this, my family let me know that, also in the fall, my dad had had a heart attack.

The months of silence made me angry. How could I possibly talk to Mom, Dad or any of my siblings? I decided I couldn't, at least not about anything important.

On that Wednesday night, I prayed this simple prayer, "Lord Jesus, when I return to campus on Monday, please send someone who will listen to all that has happened to me." This was one of the most sincere prayers I ever uttered in my life. I never dreamed God would answer in such a dramatic fashion, but He did!

Back on campus, Easter Monday, I was returning to my dorm from a late- afternoon Mass. On the path to my dorm a young woman approached and invited me to go to a Christian fellowship meeting. I said, "Sure!" But, to be honest, that was the last place I wanted to go.

After 15 or 20 minutes I convinced her to walk

alongside as I returned to my dorm in my electric wheelchair. As we went along, I began to pour out my heart. She listened with the compassion of Jesus.

When we got to my dorm, we opened my Bible to Luke 24:13-35. It was the story of Jesus' apostles meeting on the road to Emmaus. As she read the text out loud, I began to weep. God was speaking to me. That upper-classmate saved my life that night.

"Then the two recounted what had taken place on the way and how he was made known to them in the breaking of the bread" (Luke 24:35).

That night I learned, in the depths of our broken lives, we help others to meet the broken, yet resurrected Jesus. At Mass Christ comes to us through word and sacrament to live in our blemished Tabernacles, our bodies. Since that day, my life has not been the same!

SHE HOLDS ME, TOO

When I consider suffering, I do so as someone who is physically challenged. Cerebral palsy has forced me to use a wheelchair all my life. For most of my life I have believed that the suffering we bear in life is a result of the human tendency to sin.

But then I looked to Mary, who was sinless and suffered a great deal, and my argument seemed to fall apart. I found myself contemplating this problem before images of Our Lady in art, especially Michelangelo's Pietà.

There, captured in marble, we see what Mary saw: her perfect Son, broken for you and me. But I can't tell you the number of times I've looked upon the replica of Michelangelo's statue at a nearby parish Church, and, in my mind's eye, I saw Mary, holding

me in place of her beloved Son, Jesus. This masterpiece was completed in 1498 or 1499 by its sculptor
when he was 23 or 24 years old.

One night in particular, March 20, 1992, I sensed
her consolation. That night, a friend picked me up for
7 p.m. Mass. I needed to go, so that I could receive
Our Lord in Holy Communion to cope with the
reality that was suddenly before me. I had just learned
that my brother was found dead.

I sat in the back of the church, near the Pietà. And
if I closed my eyes I could see Mary holding my
brother, as I sometimes imagined her holding me. I
was comforted by my heavenly Mother as never
before.

Since then, I know why mothers who have lost sons
or daughters tend to go to Mary. She can identify with
them, and they with her. Firsthand experience helps
her identify with unwed moms, too. She knew that
humiliation. She understands.

She felt the anxiety of having her child missing.
Parents of runaways or missing children can come to
her in confidence. She understands.

She stood by as she saw her child ridiculed, falsely
accused. She understands families beset by gossip or
calumny. By her shrine, before Mass one evening, I
closed my eyes and recalled how she saved a
newlywed couple from embarrassment when they ran
out of wine. She gave the servers instructions: "Do
whatever He tells you" (see John 2:1-11). And He
turned water into wine.

If she initiated this first sign to help a couple save

face, would she allow others to spend their days on earth with a physical or mental disability alone?

I've come to believe the answer is never. In Michelangelo's Pietà, we see the depth of her acceptance, even at the death of her beloved Son. She can love us perfectly, hold us, and yet help accept our suffering, too. Mary was immaculate. Yet she suffered greatly. Perhaps it was for our sake. Simeon prophesied to Mary, when Jesus was just eight days old: "And a sword will pierce your own soul too, so that the secret thoughts of many may be laid bare" (Luke 2:35). She had already told the angel Gabriel, "Let it be done to me according to thy Word" (Luke 1:38).

In Michelangelo's masterpiece, I see a Mother who can pray for us sinners — for me, for my brothers, for my sisters and for you — now and at the hour of our death."

A NEW HOME FOR MARY

I was so excited that Christmas Eve. Never before had I been able to purchase something so beautiful for my Mom out of money I myself had earned. For the first time, I had sold a piece of writing not related to my disability to a national Catholic periodical. I wanted to use that paycheck to buy a present my Mom would treasure. And she displayed that gift in her home until the day she died. I see the Mother of God's hand in it all.

For six years I had tried to tell the story of my brother's death, but did not succeed. My strong emotions and my perfectionism always got in the way when I tried to tell the story.

So I made a promise to the Blessed Mother. "If you let me tell the story about the day my brother died, I will buy my Mom a replica of Michelangelo's 'Pieta.'" Sure enough, I got the grace to tell the story.

Still, the process of writing was long, with many revisions. But it was in telling and retelling a very personal story of faith that I was able to work through the stages of grief. I also realized in a more profound way than ever before that God uses us, his broken people, to show His Glory.

On March 20, 1992, the night of the day my brother Joe died of a drug overdose, I naturally sought consolation at a neighboring parish church. Once inside, I made my way to the church's replica of Michelangelo's "Pieta." That night I saw the Mother of Jesus in a new light.

I saw her as someone with whom I could certainly identify. The sorrow she felt was very human. It is the same depth of sorrow experienced by anyone who has lost a family member. But I saw it, too, as the sorrow of my own mother, whose anguish that night was surely at the limit of human endurance.

At that moment, Mary gave me a mirror image of my family's grief. But, from that moment, I learned to see Mary's image as a reflection of other human trials. She has helped me come to terms with my own limitations, especially my physical disability. By example, she has shown me how to accept the splinters of my cross in life. They also help me see the splinters of the cross Mary bore, and others continue to bear today.

The art of the Church has let me see the side of Mary that is vulnerable. Art is not something we worship. It is something that can help make saints or Christian heroes real to us. Of all the depictions in sacred art of Mary, the Mother of God, Michelangelo's statue "Pieta" does it best for me. It says to me, "I can unite my struggles with hers."

That's what I experienced at my brother's death in 1992. That's how I wrote the story that I finally sold in 1998. And I kept my promise. With that first paycheck, I bought my mother a replica of the "Pieta" for her living room. When she passed away earlier this year, the statue was passed on to me and took up residence in my living room.

MY FAVORITE TIME
OF THE WEEK

It is my favorite day of the week, the day I spend time before the Blessed Sacrament. Today, I have no agenda; I want Jesus to set the direction of the hour I will spend with Him.

I feel empty emotionally and need this time alone with Jesus more than most weeks. I need just to sit in the arms of the Father and let Him dictate what Jesus Christ wants of this time for me.

I think of an uncle dying of cancer. I also think about a disc jockey whose husband's health is deteriorating by the by day and a fallen president; Ronald Reagan. Like him, I felt abandoned by the Democrats.

I also pray for family and friends. Instead of

beginning this time with the Mass readings and meditation for the day, I am led to read an article on the Sacred Heart of Jesus and Saint Margaret Mary of Alacoque.

The feature reminded me of God's mercy and the countless years I was able to attend First Friday devotions. Back then, not that many years ago, a network of people were my wheels; age, death or individuals moving away has ebbed that network like the ocean does to its shore. The article, made me remember those days fondly. I miss them, though I don't miss the wee hours of the morning I came home each month after the long evening out.

The monthly devotions opened with a Mass to the Sacred Heart at 9 PM and concluded with a Mass to the Immaculate Heart of Mary at mid-night. Devotional prayers were said and Confessions were heard between the two Masses.

One of my intention's each month was that a long winded priest wouldn't say the closing Eucharistic Liturgy. Usually God had a deaf ear to that request. Thinking about that today brings a smile to my face.

Do to my disability others would have to wait up for me to come home. The longer the evening was the guiltier I felt for keeping a family member awake.

Today, my devotion is more private. Adoration once a week as well as reflecting on the daily mass readings and using a well known Scriptural guide for meditation on the rosary daily and weekly mass is all I can do.

Paratransit is a transportation system for the

disabled. These days it is my main means of travel. With its use, I feel a sense of independence. One of the weekly trips I schedule is a roundtrip to my parish for time before the Blessed Sacrament.

With the church nearly empty I dump my concerns before Our Lord. Whether I tell Christ my concerns in silence or mention them aloud is unimportant. Like the apostles in their first holy hour the day before Christ was condemned to death; my time is not always fruitful. I may sleep or be distracted, nevertheless, I am there and God knows the intention of my heart.

Since the year 2000 I can count on one hand the number of weeks I have missed my time of Adoration. Jesus awaits that visit. He knows it has become my favorite time of the week!

A DATE WITH OUR
BLESSED LORD

It is Thursday, November 13, 2008. Thanksgiving is two weeks away. Saturday evening after Mass I made a date at this time to be with Our Lord; it is a date I feel more urgent to keep since the election results earlier this month.

I feel it will be important to make the trip to Washington this coming January. I must begin to pray for the success of the March for Life early. A freak injury during last year's march may have deterred me from going this January, but Obama's election has made it critical that I go despite the fact that during last year's March for Life my left knee was injured. The weather can't play a factor in my decision. Frigid cold and my spastic body may limit my ability to bend when temperatures are less than moderate. When it is cold my flexibility decreases dramatically. I prayed it was an unusually warm day. Therefore, with the temperature below freezing and much of the day's activities outdoors, I didn't give my decision to go to the church another thought.

Without considering these factors, one could rightly state I would have been acting selfishly. Therefore, my Adoration time over the next few months will be that Jesus changes the heart of the President-elect.

Remembering the Anniversary

It will be thirty-six years ago; the date was January 22, 1973. On that day the U.S. Supreme Court legalized abortion, the lawful killing of the unborn in a Mother's womb. It was just the beginning of America's slippery slope into a culture of death into which we are still descending.

Having a disability since my birth has forced me to allow others to be my arms and legs. In allowing them to help me maybe I have helped them to work out their salvation and encounter Christ!

On this day, at Adoration, I recall the words of Bishop Sheen that "we are all cracked pots." Time and again throughout my life, God has affirmed these words of the late bishop. Those who are broken have assisted me. In the broken, God indeed shows His Glory!

My date with Our Lord was for the most part spent in silence. I wept also in silence for the tremendous loss of life over the last thirty-five years. In that time, I have prayed for the millions of children killed since that fateful day, January 22, 1973. That time at Adoration was a time of reparation; I offered the splinters of my cross for unwed moms who have to have the courage to stand for life. I also prayed for the women victimized by abortion. Lord, let the witness of our lives change the hearts of those moms whose unborn children's lives are at risk.

Lord, give us the courage to risk to move forward by reaching out to someone who is an outcast of our society; the disabled, the elderly or someone on death row. By our actions let us transform this culture of death into a culture of life.

I Seek Our Lord's Forgiveness

Lord, forgive me for the times I have not taken action. Forgive me for the times I have not reflected a respect for all human life. Forgive me for the times I turned people away from the truth by my zeal or lack of it. Transform me so that people will see the difference you've made in my life. Lord, let my witness give them a desire to follow you.

I meditated on the Mass Readings of the day, said the Rosary, and ended my visit with "the Divine Praises" as well as this prayer:

Lord, as I close this time before the Blessed Sacrament, I ask that each day I spend in a wheelchair, by your grace help bring a soul to heaven! Since I spend 12-16 hours a day, in this renewed commitment to offer up my suffering for you Christ, help me lead others to you.

Lord, thank you for making this date with you very fruitful. In your kindness allow my silent witness to trigger one woman not to abort her unborn child this day. If this happens, by your grace, I will have known the hours spent in my wheelchair this day were not in vein.

As I transfer from my wheelchair to my hospital bed, these thoughts give my mind, if not the bottom I've been sitting on all day, much needed comfort.

MY FAVORITE
MYSTERY OF LIGHT

October is a month dedicated to Our Blessed Mother. During this month in 20002, Pope John Paul II introduced the Luminous Mysteries of the Rosary. A few months before his passing, as the Church was completing the celebration of its "Year of the Eucharist," I felt this was an ideal time to get acquainted with the Mysteries of Light; and so I did. These five mysteries of the rosary focus on some of the important public events of Christ's life.

When the late Pope John Paul II introduced the Luminous Mysteries in October of 2002, I asked myself "why update this treasure of the Church?" After all, I reasoned, I had been reintroduced this treasure of the Church and was comfortable meditating on the Rosary with a Scriptural Rosary book I had been using for years. This tool had brought the meaning of this prayer form to life for me after college.

I asked myself, "Why get away from something that brought the mysteries of the rosaries alive for you?" Nevertheless, after my initial reaction I was driven to begin a personal search for a suitable replacement for my trusted Scriptural Rosary Book. I wanted a book that included meditations on the new Mysteries of Light. The search took me some time; nearly two years. The end result was well worth the effort. This find has given me new insight as to the wisdom of the Holy Father behind his introducing the additional set of five rosary mysteries; "The Baptism of Christ in the Jordon, "The Wedding at Cana," "The Proclaiming of the Kingdom," "The Transfiguration" and "The Institution of the Eucharist."

I have even come to have a favorite Mystery of Light. The Luminous Mystery I am speaking of is the Fifth Luminous Mystery; the Institution of the Eucharist. Each time I meditate on this decade of the rosary, I am taken to the upper room where Christ shared that last meal with His friends. I meditate on this mystery of the rosary and I have gained a deeper understanding and love of the Blessed Sacrament. In this one mystery I have also come to realize the wisdom of the Holy Father in creating the Mysteries of Light.

This mystery of the holy rosary is like a spiritual communion for me. Each time I meditate on its meaning, I think of the depth of Christ's love for us. Just think about it; at that last meal, Christ instituted a way He could be with us always! Yes, until the end of time.

At that first Mass, the last meal Christ shared with his disciples, he transformed bread and wine into His Body and Blood. He said, "Each time you do this, do it in memory of me."

Reflecting on the Fifth Luminous Mystery has been an ideal way for me to begin my time before the Blessed Sacrament each week.

As this special year of the Church was celebrated, I give thanks to God for our late Holy Father as well as his successor, Benedict the XVI, and recalled their love for the rosary.

Each week during Adoration, I ask the Holy Spirit to guide me as I reflect on the Luminous Mysteries. I challenge you to do the same!

As you reflect on this mystery, I pray it gives all of us a greater love and reverence for Mass and the Eucharist as the late Holy Father intended to happen. During the year he dedicated it to the holy rosary we were asked to reflect on this Most Blessed Sacrament; such a prayer will never go unanswered!

A WONDERFUL FLIGHT HIGHLIGHTS A REMARKABLE WEEK

I was 49 years old at the time, it was 2003, and generally at the time I spent up to 16 hours a day in my wheelchair. I am dependent on others to bathe, dress and shave me. At times I feel like a puppet at the whims of others. My dependency on others due my disability affects the extent of my involvement with social, political as well as religious activities. Therefore, when I had the chance to do something in which I was in control or free of someone else's good will I seriously considered the opportunity. And I am glad I did! My Mom's recent death had me thinking back to a trip down the shore in August of 2003; a vacation in which Mom was with us.

For Some Background

I have spastic cerebral palsy. At times my body can be as flexible as a Clear Channel, Infinity Broadcasting or Greater Media formatted Radio Station. Therefore even with a blue sky, a gentle breeze, and temperatures in the mid-seventies, this made that Friday a perfect day to Para-sail, there was still much at risk for me. If I thought about it too much, I would back out!

Weather sometimes plays a part in my body's stiffness, but it is not the only factor that contributes to body's flexibility. Most apprehension about doing something new can also contribute my to body's stiffness. With this as a backdrop, I'd like to give you an account of my adventure of one August day.

Journal Notes

"It is Friday, August 22, 2003, the last full day of our vacation. With nine other family members present, I was lifted out of my wheelchair by my brother-in-law Mike and boarded a boat to Para-sail. The nine others did the same. My nephew Justin, 16, and I were among the last to take flight." As I went up with my nephew, my leg had a spasm.

"Though I needed to be carried onto the chute, the experience was one in which I felt I had complete freedom. In the chute, I was an equal to those who ventured with me to rise 500 feet above the ocean.

This was a two-hour boat ride for all of us. The ten-minute flight included in that trip was the highlight of my week down the shore. For those ten minutes I was in the air able to forget my own physical limitations. My stomach seemed to leave me and had a spasm for a moment as I was lifted up. Thank God, it stopped."

I held on for dear life as I looked at the ocean below. This was a Kodak moment and it was mine. Overjoyed, I felt like I had pitched and won the deciding game of the World Series.

Like everyone I had a lifejacket and parachute put on me. Unlike most of the adults, I wore my lifejacket throughout the two-hour boat ride. This was due to the fact of the difficulty I have in keep my balance without something to grip. As an added precaution, I took a seat on the end, so, I could hold on to the boat's rail.

If there were any regrets that I have about the entire experience, it would be a small one; hardly worth mentioning. It is the fact that my nephew Justin and I weren't given the option to dip our feet into the ocean as we ascended back into the boat. Understandably, the boat operator thought it was a safety risk.

I realize if it weren't for my faith, what became the highlight of our family vacation for me, I wouldn't have dared to parasail! Though I did many other things during the week, parasailing will stick in my memory.

In those few moments, I was able to forget my dependency on others, with help of a day's gentle wind I felt like a puppet with no strings.

Yes, for the rest of the ride on the boat I felt like Pinocchio, totally free! The moment I was placed in my wheelchair, I felt emotionally drained as I was brought down earth; yet, I was happy; for I knew, I had a great story to tell!

Like Peter, James and John had at the Transfiguration, on that August day, I had my own mountaintop experience!

FROM MORN TO NIGHT

There are so many people who allow me to be a functioning human being. I can't thank them all, but without their assistance I could not get through a single day. They are the arms and legs that help me with the tasks of daily living from shaving, dressing and even preparing meals. They even help me with toileting.

It is 5:45 A.M. I have had a restless night of sleep at best waking up several times to go to bathroom. Thank God, a hand urinal is on the side rail of my hospital bed. By this time I give up on sleeping and put EWTN on the television. I have an hour and a half until my friend will dress me and prepare me to go to the funeral Mass of a dear friend.

The Church was packed with people who had been

touched by this humble woman of faith. This woman touched many lives. She lived the Beatitudes. The priest who eulogized her said, "She had the spirit of Mother Teresa." What I know is that when you spoke with her it was as if you were the only one in the room.

I know her entire family. Her children and husband are among the finest people I know. I would kick myself if I had not made the effort, though it meant rushing to my optometrist when I came home.

I smile as I think of God's timing. My attendant quickly washed and dressed me and the two of us were on our way. It would take 45 minutes. The return trip would only take 35 minutes. Gabriel, my attendant, noted, "It is easier to push down hill!" This Godsend from Haiti has been there for me for over seven years. I call him my "Christmas Angel" since he came to me in December of 2000.

The next day a friend who works for me on weekends and has been there for me in times of emergency walked beside me to morning Mass. I like Saturdays, because my day usually begins and ends with Mass and reception of Holy Communion. Despite anything else that happens during the day - the Mass and the Eucharist make the burdens of the day easier to bear.

When we come back from Mass and Dunkin' Donuts, a Saturday ritual, I must ask this young man to help me on the toilet. And, yes, when I'm finished the man wipes my bottom. This friend doesn't complain. His help at this moment is an act of God's grace which shows through him. Though, I am a man of 53, this need makes me feel like a child of three about to get spanked as I bend over to get wiped. For me, it is one of the most humiliating parts of the day.

For lunch I have a pork chop, mixed vegetables and apple sauce that are given to me by a group called Aid For Friends. It is coordinated with the help of various churches and denominations, including the local Catholic Parishes. Every time I eat one of their homemade meals, I ask God to bless those who share of their bounty or perhaps of their want. For we don't know the life circumstances of those that contribute meals or give of their time to deliver them.

I eat these prepared meals at lunch due in part to the fact that someone is there to help me cook those meals. I also don't like to go bed with a heavy stomach. Around 3 PM a prayer partner and I pray the Rosary over the phone.

Upon retuning from the Saturday Vigil Mass, I have a surprise visit from my sister Rosemary and her husband Mike. Their visit means I won't have to wait until after ten that evening to get in bed. Mike helps me transfer from my power chair to my hospital bed.

As I reflect on the day about to end, I am amazed at the number of people who have directly or indirectly impacted my life today. For that matter whom I may have made an impact on myself.

WITH HELP FROM GOD
& NEW FRIENDS

There is a wonderful song from the musical of stage and screen "Carousel" entitled "You'll Never Walk Alone" and this is true. God's people are interdependent on one another. God has been emphasizing this point in my life at this time, particularly over the last few months. He has shown me how He has been working in my life in a powerful way. As I thumbed through my prayer journal, a reflection from the day I moved into this apartment brings home that point and illustrates just how powerfully His hand has touched and blest my life. I would love to share this with you. It was written in a spirit of true thanksgiving.

It was November 23, 2005. Three months from the

day I moved into this apartment complex. It was
summer then.   Today's weather gave us a winter
preview, if not a complete immersion into the season.
However, according to my calendar, the Season of
Winter is nearly a month away.   So, as I write this
journal entry I realize, though I have moved out on
my own, my support system hasn't weakened or
abandoned me. Nor has God.

In fact, if anything, my dependency on my network
of support as well as my dependency on God, has
really strengthened and grown becoming more
important to my very survival.

Tomorrow an automatic door-opener will be
installed.   It will greatly enhance my freedom and
greatly reduce my dependency on others.   But, in
truth, God has blessed me with this time of greater
dependency on many wonderful people.   Though I
have kicked and screamed over the delays, I now see
His hand in the whole process.

Throughout my life God has placed people in my
life to help me on my journey. That is also true at this
phase of my journey. Even though I complain, God
faithfully provides people who become my arms and
legs so that I may not merely exist, but live!

One of those people is a woman of deep courage
who is on the waiting list for a kidney.   She is the
apartment complex's chief cook, a member of
council, as well as a faithful wife, mother and
grandmother. This courageous woman has seen to it
that I have gotten to whatever activities I wanted to
attend. If she did not personally escort me, she would

designate someone to do so. I pray she gets her kidney.

Another person who has been there for me is an extraordinary 49-year-old widow. A young woman, who has the gift of gab, but also an extremely keen ability to listen, and has been my anchor. Like me, though not as severe as mine, this woman has a form of spastic cerebral palsy. Like me, it is this woman's faith that gets her through the struggles of a given day.

Then, there is another remarkable woman who is 92. She spends her days crocheting lap blankets for disabled veterans. Weeks after my arrival I received one of these works of love from this pious lady after meeting her during the community's Tuesday evening Rosary group.

I also want to mention a man who rides a limousine. He volunteers to bring home meals prepared by people I will never meet. The food is delicious—and who can put a price on weekly visits as we share laughter, tears and a little of what has gone on in each of our lives. This great storyteller has come into my life thanks to "AID FOR FRIENDS." Both the food and weekly visits are priceless blessings.

I know two young girls that have recently become pen pals. It is great that they share so easily about their faith and lives. I hope their fire for doing so never dies. One of those wrote me about a book on early martyrs of the Church including Saint Agnes. "The book was a wonderful read written by Cardinal

Wiseman."

With an endorsement like that who could resist picking it and adding it to their summer must read list. With youth on fire for Our Blessed Lord like the two young ladies I am speaking of how could I help but think of days such as these anything but a blessing!

In each case mentioned, as well as countless others, individuals have treated me like family. With help from these new friends, this new apartment has truly become a home, my home; a home where all are welcome!

By these examples, one can see it is true that the people who make a difference in your life are not the ones with the most credentials, the most money, or the most awards. They are the ones that care.

A GRATEFUL HEART

Recently, I spoke at our local YMCA. The date was May 13th, the Feast of Our Lady of Fatima. That day, I certainly felt under Mary's protection as I said a silent "Hail Mary" before speaking and prayed a Rosary earlier that morning. I was asked to speak weeks earlier, as I was cornered in the Men's room by the YMCA' S CEO.

My speech was brief, but sincere. I began my talk with words similar to those spoken by St. Peter at the Transfiguration. As I thought about St. Paul's words as he offered to build three tents "Lord, it is good that we are here." (See Mark 9:2-8) I paraphrased him as I began by stating, "It is a gift from God that I am here today."

I went on to say:

The scholarship program has not only allowed me to benefit physically, but in the process I have developed both emotionally and spiritually as an individual. Recognizing this allows me to stretch my expectations giving me the opportunity to be in full gear to set new and greater goals for myself as time passes.

I paused then said:

Friends and acquaintances have pushed me farther than I ever dreamed possible. It is as if the competition has been a great source of motivation for me, the kind of drive I lacked in my youth. Let me correct that, my drive was going in a different direction; namely, education. For I thought at the time education would mean freedom despite my disability.

Then I made a big mistake, I began mentioning names. I know that is a bottomless pit. Because, I am sure I forgot someone. Despite this fact, I didn't lose my audience (though I lost control of my emotions). To my surprise, as I concluded, I received a standing ovation.

With the two paragraphs below, I concluded my testimonial:

People like Gary, Eric, Cindy, Gabriel and

lastly Martha have all played a role in my
success here. They have encouraged me in
countless ways and have been there to lift me in
times of doubt. Their support and the support of
so many others have made all the difference.

This said I am glad our God is a God of second or
numerous chances. He understands the season we are
at now in our life. The YMCA has been very much a
part of my personal growth in this season of my life
and for that I have a grateful heart.

As I reflect on the words I had spoken that day, I
realize I should have provided tissues for all who were
present. The CEO later told me "Bill, there was not a
dry eye in the house!" I am not afraid or ashamed to
admit I cried too.

A couple weeks later, I put legs to words of
gratitude by making a monthly pledge to the YMCA.
Though it may seem like a drop in the bucket to some
on a fixed income, it was large amount to me. It
reminds me of the widow's contribution in the
Synagogue or Temple (see Mark 12:41-44). Jesus let
those present know that this widow had given from
her poverty. The last verse of the story makes it clear.

For they have all contributed from their
surplus wealth, but she, from her poverty, has
contributed all she had, her whole livelihood.

Like the widow in the story in this passage from Mark, I gave my pledge to the YMCA out of my limited resources. No way could I match the contributions of the donors present, but my donation did stem from a grateful heart!

WE SAID GOOD-BYE TO A GREAT PRIEST AND A GOOD FRIEND

There have been so many negative things written about priests in recent years that I am glad I am able in this column to pay tribute to a priest who dedicated his life to his Church and his country. He was a faithful servant, a dear friend, a real role-model to old and young alike.

Father Henry Dougherty, a retired priest and resident at Villa St. Joseph in Darby died on Thursday, May 12, 2005. He was born October 1, 1914. He was 90. Father Dougherty was ordained June 7, 1941, at the Cathedral of SS. Peter and Paul by Cardinal Dennis Dougherty. For more than a quarter-century I knew this holy man. I can't help but think the community has lost a good priest, but just as importantly America has lost yet another one of what Tom Brokaw has called its "Greatest Generation."

It was when Father Dougherty was stationed at Queen of the Universe in Levittown as a parochial vicar (1980-90) that I came to know this priest. He remained there in residence after his retirement until 2001

Other assignments included parochial vicar at All Saints Chapel, St. James Parish and St. Timothy Parish, Philadelphia as well as St. Alice Parish, Upper Darby. .

Anyone who knew him knew this holy man had a deep love for Mass and the Sacraments and in particular Reconciliation and the Eucharist. He was a gifted storyteller and great homilist. I always felt blessed when I lectored or attended one of his Masses. For I knew not only would I be fed with the Body and Blood of Christ, but also would be fed with his spiritual wisdom.

A striking impression one could easily get at every Mass he served was his love of children. Adults brought their young ones up who were not old enough to receive Jesus in the Eucharist were blessed on the forehead by this wonderful priest. He loved children.

Therefore, I was not surprised to read that he taught members of his family how to drive a car. He also took his nieces and nephews down the shore. Family was important to him. Father Dougherty also took his priestly duties seriously.

I know from personal experience that Father

Dougherty was great Confessor. He would pull things out of me that would make me want to change. He could read hearts. Absolution was not automatic with him. This is one of the reasons; I loved and respected this holy man.

I was in a giddy mood one day, something had struck me funny. The grin on my face unmasked the fact that in wasn't in proper frame of mind for the Sacrament of Reconciliation; but I tried. After several attempts, we both gave up. Since that day, I always try to go to Confession with a contrite spirit.

At his funeral Mass I found out that this priest was an Army Chaplain from 1943-47. He also was a paratrooper. During that time, he was interviewed and asked by a reporter, "Is true when someone from a plane they say "Geronimo?"

Father Paul Wiedmann, the homilist for the Mass gave Father Dougherty's response, "I can't speak for others, but as me, each time I jump, I say An Act of Contrition" As the story was told at the funeral Mass at Queen of the Universe in a moving eulogy, laughter broke out. The story was recounted in a fitting tribute the following week in Philadelphia's Catholic Standard & Times.

Father Dougherty "you are a priest forever" and I am glad your ministry touched my life. I was also glad your funeral Mass was at a Church I call my second spiritual home. I was honored to be there.

SPEND AN HOUR WITH ME

Today, as I spend time before the Blessed Sacrament, I think of many things. One of those things I think about is the fact that several years ago someone sent me a book when I had doubts in Christ's True Presence in the Eucharist. The book was "Miracle of the Eucharist" by Bob and Penny Lord. For me, the accounts in this book dispelled all doubts. And I was transformed from a Catholic who just went to mass weekly, to a person who lives his faith daily.

Over the pass two and a half years, this commitment to my faith has included weekly Adoration. I have been faithful to that commitment making a weekly Visit on all but few weeks over that period of time. Still, Church Feast Days, like the one approaching us reminds me why I need to make such

Visits.

It is June. The Church has dedicated this month to the Sacred Heart of Jesus. We are also approaching the Feast of Corpus Christi, which literally translated means the Body and Blood of Christ.

The Gospel on This Feast

The Gospel Reading to be used (Mark 14:12-16; 22-26) on the Feast, Sunday, June 22, 2003 ends with the group going to the Mount of Olives. The entire passage reminds us of the lasting gift Christ gave us at the Last Supper. We often hear these words during mass, but do realize their impact! With a little reflection, one can see how in Christ's actions that night he fulfilled the promise quoted at the end of Matthew's Gospel "I will be with you until the end of time." Think about it, many of the Apostles, who ran scared the next day, became martyrs of the faith.

They had hope in Christ's promise and proof on their Altars. His fulfillment of the just mentioned promise is an awesome thought! Each time we attend mass we can share what the Apostles shared at that Holy Thursday Supper the Body, Blood, Soul and Divinity of Jesus.

What a gift He gave that night? Yet, regardless of when I come to Visit, few people are there. It is too often just He and I alone. Yet, I am grateful the flexibility of my schedule affords this privilege each week.

Instead of judging others, I am thankful I have this chance. As I think about this fact, I feel overwhelmed by Christ's peace. Yet, I also feel so unworthy to be in His presence.

I then meditate on this gospel reading at Adoration. It reminds me that Christ's Real presence on the Altar is worth spending time each week. Though every visit may not be fruitful, I am among saints. His own Apostles' failed Him on their first Holy Hour; on the very night before he died!

They couldn't stay awake and pray with Jesus. They couldn't honor his request of them "Spend an Hour with me." Sacred Scripture records they fell asleep. I am reminded that on occasions, I too have fallen asleep at times during my time before the Blessed Sacrament. By faithfully going to Adoration, I can make up for the times I have been there in body, but not in spirit.

Peter, the first Pope, denied you, Christ, three times. Yet, Jesus, you called him the "rock" and called him to lead your Church. As I take this moment to pray for the man who sits on the Chair of Peter.

Thank you for his love for the youth of the world. Let his witness inspire many of them to lives of holiness. Thank you for his witness in showing how to offer our suffering. Thank you for his witness in reaching out to others.

By not reaching out to others in need, how often have I denied you? Lord, truly present on the Altar, forgive me for times I have not done what I could have done for others. Forgive me for the times I have been judgmental or harsh when viewing the actions of others.

This Feast, this month dedicated to the Sacred Heart reminds us of the price Christ paid for our sins. It is an opportunity to recommit our lives to Christ and renew the love we had for this Sacrament as a child. Take up my challenge and spend an hour with Him.

A BOOK REVIEW

The Extraordinary Life & Legacy of Archbishop Noll: Champion of the Church by Ann Ball with Father Leon Hutton published by Our Sunday Visitor 200 Noll Plaza, Huntington, IN. 48750 Copyright 2006 . Paperback, 144 pages, $14.95.

A Man of Faith's Vision and Legacy Is Told
Wonderfully in This New Tribute

All of us have dreams and ideas, John Francis Noll was no exception. He had the good fortune and God-given ability and foresight to turn his into reality. This wonderfully written little book has been published just in time to commemorate the 50th anniversary of the death of this Bishop and pioneer of Catholic publishing. As I read about this man of faith that fought bigotry, prejudice and anti-Catholicism head-on in his day through educating Catholics and non-Catholics alike on the truths of our faith, I asked myself, "Am I not called to the same?"

Since the laity interacts daily with non-Catholics we have a greater opportunity to lead others to the fullness of our faith more so than the priest. This having been said, this holy man was aware Catholics and Protestants alike are not well versed in the tenants of faith. This was a great part of his mission as a priest, bishop and publisher.

Through his life's work he showed the world that one "could be a good Catholic and a good American," Bishop Noll certainly did. He saw the increasing role of the laity prior to Vatican II. In an early chapter readers discover:

John Noll had his roots firmly planted deep in the Indiana soil. The Noll family had settled in this sleepy little farming community in 1834, when his grandfather, George Johannes Noll, a tailor, emigrated from Germany. The family rode in a wagon from Detroit Michigan over an almost impossible road, as there was no railroad or waterway to get to Fort Wayne.

His father, John George Noll, one of three brothers, was born in 1841. John's mother, Anna Ford, was born in London, England of Irish parents in 1843. She came to America as a young girl and married John George about 1864. The young couple immediately began to raise a family. John George held a number of occupations: he ran a haberdashery, worked as a grocer, and at one time was a bookkeeper for the city comptroller for the city of Fort Wayne. He also served as councilman. Anna had her hands full with the care of the babies who arrived almost annually..." (Chapter 2, paragraphs 1 and 2).

The sentence concluded by naming the Noll children in order of their birth. This future Archbishop and defender of the faith was the sixth of seven children. John was born on January 25, 1875; in the house next door to the house where his father was born.

A week later he was baptized at the same Cathedral church in Fort Wayne, as his father had been thirty-four-years earlier. Indeed, his roots were deeply planted in the rich soil of Indiana.

His mother's death when he was 3 ½ years-old and his father's marriage a year later to a woman who was Protestant helped young John understand from an early age the importance of teaching the tenets of our faith to Catholics and non-Catholics alike. John's stepmother, Mary, became a convert to Catholicism. Her conversion sparked a lifelong interest in bringing new souls into the fold of the Catholic Church.

A pioneer in publishing, this founder of Our Sunday Visitor newspaper and publishing company was bold enough to use the latest technical advances of the day. Today the company this dedicated priest founded is doing the same with its use of CD-ROMs as well as the Internet.

Reading this book one reads about the life of a man, who knew his mission in life and went about

fulfilling it and Catholics are better educated due to
the publishing company this great priest and bishop
founded as well as his vision for the laity, apostles
and teachers of the faith. Ann Ball and her team of
researchers say it well:

"In his time, Bishop Noll was to the printed word
what Bishop Fulton Sheen was to the spoken one; to
this day, he remains the outstanding Catholic
publisher America has ever known (concluding
paragraph page 68).

His was a remarkable faith journey and the
publishing company he founded is honoring him with
this touching tribute 50 years after his death. It is
great read.

A DREAM COME TRUE

It is silent as I enter the church. I feel alone with my thoughts and God. There are others here, but I am isolated with the burdens and prayers I have on my heart. I know so many hurting people. What do I say? How do I react to the awe I feel in Christ's presence? How do I thank Him for what He has done for me? Being here, able to pour out my soul, my deepest concerns in the Presence of the Lord, is a dream come true.

It is a freedom many of us take for granted. Admittedly, I have done so in the past. Yet, I know, the God, present before me on the altar, knows my heart. All I have to do is to ask for His forgiveness for those times I have needed it, to accept that forgiveness and to be bathed in His Ocean of mercy.

I wept, overwhelmed, as I realized the depth of Christ's selflessness. His very presence here in the Blessed Sacrament is witness to this truth. The reality of the corpse of Christ on the cross, the Crucifix in front of the Church is another reminder of depth of Christ's love. The Stations' of the Cross on the side walls of the church are yet another reminder of Christ's sacrifice for us; His Life, His Death and His Resurrection are all examples for us.

It is Thursday, as such, a part of the time I spend here will be reflecting on the Mysteries of Light; a gift given to the Church by Pope John Paul II. These five mysteries of the Rosary focus on the Public Ministry of Christ's Life; namely, His Baptism, The Wedding at Cana, The Proclamation of the Kingdom, The Transfiguration and lastly, The Institution of the Eucharist! They are beautiful things to reflect on with the help of sacred scripture.

These mysteries gave me a renewed enthusiasm for reciting the Rosary when they were introduced by the late Holy Father and they lift my spirits each time I meditate on them. His insight for knowing there was a need for them must have been inspired by God and the Blessed Mother.

Fittingly, I dedicate or unite my sufferings each Thursday on behalf of priests who have lost their way. These men are blest to give birth to Christ each day at Mass; while Mary only did it once.

Mary's "Yes" to the angel Gabriel, allowed the dream of Our Father in heaven to come true.

THE SIX PACK

Though the Phillies lost in round two of the National League playoff in 2010 to the San Francisco Giants, fans didn't have much time to wallow in their sorrows. Full and partial season tickets went on sale in November and this year, for the first time, the Phillies offered a six game package.

I have been a lifetime baseball fan and have been on board with the Phillies since early childhood. I recall in the 1960's having Jim Bunning pajamas. The pajama's top back bore his name and number 14.

On Father's Day 1964, this boyhood hero pitched a perfect game. From that day on I dreamed of becoming a sports broadcaster. My dreams included interviewing players like Bunning after a huge victory. Though, physical limitations have prevented me from fully living out that dream, God has given me some special moments associated with baseball, its stars and the print media.

Several years ago I moved into my own apartment. Something I never dreamed would be possible for me as person with a physical disability: spastic cerebral palsy. Nevertheless, it happened! And, this year, another lifelong dream of mine has come true. I and a friend have purchased a pair of tickets for six games. We dreamed of being Phillies season ticket holders. Well, this year it happened, Sharing the expense with each other, we were able to purchase the tickets for a six pack of games; 12 tickets for six businessperson specials. We are both disabled and use wheelchairs for mobility.

We finished our package of Phillies games with three wins and three losses. Their overall record to date was 83-45. On August 24th my friend and I attended our last game of this season. That game was against the New York Mets. The Phillies lost 7-4.

Despite problems with transportation, the weather as well as my personal bathroom issues, I know, we feel blessed we were able to buy the tickets. For us personally, this six pack of tickets, have given us more than a few afternoons of enjoyment. It has allowed us to have a lifelong dream of ours to come true; be partial season ticket holder. We have been given the chance to boo, cheer or just plain get excited like any other fans. For those few hours we are able not to focus on our disability. For three hours or more we are one in the crowd. In other words, just get into the game!

Thank you, young lady. I love you. Our Christmas present to each other has made this one of the most memorable summers of my life!

I pray all the readers of this column have a safe Labor Day Weekend and perhaps might be inspired to purchase a six pack of tickets for a baseball team near you.

JOY ON WHEELS

I saw a chance to "do small things with great love," as Blessed Mother Teresa urged — and took it.

I went to my favorite bookstore the other day. This is not a newsflash since I go there once or twice a month. While there, I like to observe the interaction between the children and the adults. There's something about the interplay between experience and discovery that I find both fascinating and formative.

During this visit, I hit the jackpot. A young woman had charge of four preschoolers, all girls. Two were hers while the others were her sister's. The woman, I quickly noticed, treated all the same. She showed no favoritism.

The woman entertained the kids in the café at a

table near were I was sitting. She seemed to have an endless supply of goodies in her bag — Cheerios, fruits, crackers.

The bag she carried seemed like something out of *Mary Poppins.* It was more like a bottomless pit than a purse. That was good, as the children's appetites proved the bag's match. And the woman's patience matched her children's appetites. I thought: "This humble woman, who clearly takes much joy in caring for kids, is a saint."

In the course of an hour or so, she told one of the children at least a dozen times to sit still. I believe she was worried about the child falling off the chair. Each time, as soon as the woman lifted and sat the child back down, the little girl would start fidgeting dangerously close to the edge again.

From her bottomless bag, the woman soon produced a book — the Dr. Seuss classic *Green Eggs and Ham.* The reading of this whimsical tale calmed the 4-year-old down. She quickly became gripped by the story of a stubborn eccentric who found it hard to try something new.

"Mommy," said the child, "I don't like to try new things either." The woman leaned over the table, gave the child a hug and said, with a twinge of laughter in her voice: "Don't I know it!"

When the woman's sister returned, the one tending the children stepped out of the store for a moment. In a couple of minutes she re-entered, pushing a child-size wheelchair. She placed the little squirmer in the chair and took her for a ride through the store.

In that moment, I saw myself as a child again. I, too, was born with a disability that confined me to a wheelchair. And I, too, was stubborn and fidgety.

A little later, the group landed right behind my wheelchair in the cashier's line. I paid for my purchase as well as the special child's book. As far as I know, I'm not a saint. I was just living out some lessons Blessed Teresa of Calcutta taught with her words as well as her life:

"Joy is a net of love by which you can catch souls. … If we have no peace, it is because we have forgotten that we belong to each other." And of course, "In this life we cannot do great things. We can only do small things with great love."

While waiting for my transportation, I saw that little girl holding the huge Barney book I'd just treated her to. She was now wearing a smile so broad it would put big Barney's toothy grin to shame. As her mother thanked me with tears of gratitude, I thought: "That smile is all the thanks I needed." Well, that and the chance to add someone new to my list of souls to pray for.

A LOOK AT MY WEEKEND

In Memory of Dick Clark, 1929-2012

It was a Saturday in early November of 2010 that I got reacquainted with a radio program I had grown to love over the years. It is hosted by a legend of the music industry: Dick Clark. This program "Rock, Roll & Remember" airs 6-10 A.M. on WIBG FM 94.3 out of Ocean City, New Jersey and 14 other radio stations throughout the nation. The program had been a highlight of my weekend for several years. Not long ago it was through the wonder of the Internet that this re-connection occurred. To my regret, WOGL FM, the local station that once carried this syndicated program for a number of years dropped it a few years ago.

Though it is broadcast an hour later than when it aired on WOGL, 6 in the morning on a Saturday is still quite early. Nevertheless, a true fan of the program's host, I try not to miss a moment. After all, the program's host, Dick Clark, is one of the rock era's most knowledgeable personalities. When he tells the stories behind the music, it makes me, as a listener, feel as if I were on the lap of an uncle, aunt, parent or grandparent who is sharing firsthand accounts from the wealth of his life experiences. And in this case, who is better qualified to host such a program than Dick Clark, the longtime host of "American Bandstand," the man who introduced America to many of the artists featured on this rock anthology program? In this nation, I say no one!

For me, the show is my weekly stroll through the music which has become so much a part of the soundtrack of my life. I did not have many records, and my spastic cerebral palsy did not allow me to keep the ones I did have in good condition. Therefore, I use the time as an escape from the struggles of the week that was ending and tune out from the worries and concerns of the upcoming week, simply recalling the hours I spent as a child listening to one of the radio personalities playing or introducing the music of the day.

Clark was one of those personalities. Each Saturday morning is like a religious experience connecting me with my past. With those radio personalities going the way of World War II veterans, I sense an era dying. I know this is a big reason why, though music is often in the background as I work, seldom do I listen as intently as I do on any given Saturday morning.

Is it any wonder then this early morning ritual helps me prepare for that evening's Mass? Let me explain. My office in the living room is some distance from my bedroom. Therefore, I set my computer to WIBG 94.3 each Friday night. I have to turn it up so that I don't miss the stories behind the music each Saturday morning. This fact forces me to concentrate on the details. The sound system in the Church depending where I sit forces me to concentrate intently also.

If listening to Dick Clark is a highlight of my Saturday morning, I would say Saturday evening Mass is the summit of my week. It is where I worship, along with the parish community, and together we affirm our faith.

It is where we hear and are called to respond to the Word of God as it is proclaimed and explained. It is where we profess our beliefs by reciting the ancient creed of our Church.

Then we celebrate the sacred meal, and remember the night Christ took bread in His sacred hands, blessed it, broke it gave it to His disciples telling them, "This is my body...do this in memory of me."

In like fashion Christ took the Cup, said a blessing and gave it to them saying, "this is my Blood...shed for many. Do this in remembrance of Me." As a Catholic, I see this as a sign Christ has kept His promise "I will be with you always until the end of time." All of us in Christ's body are broken and blessed, wounded yet strengthened by the whole of our life experience. At each Mass, we share the gift of ourselves. After all, this is what we bring to His banquet — our entire being, warts and all. On the night Christ was betrayed, broken, yet blessed, He emptied Himself. Having given His all, He gave us no less; in the form of bread and wine, we receive His Body, Blood, Soul and Divinity. It was fitting that, in Matthew 22:1-14, Jesus likened the kingdom of heaven to "a wedding feast." Lord, let us accept the invitation. As a Catholic, one can read this banquet in the Gospel reading as a metaphor for the Mass.

My Saturday may begin with a legend in the music industry, but before my day ends with dinner with family or friends or more often than not by myself. I celebrate the sacred feast which embodies the life, passion death and resurrection of Christ; namely, the holy sacrifice of the Mass.

It is fitting that I do it in the middle of my weekend, for Christ should be the Center of my life. As a human being, given my fallen nature, I can't say that I always keep Him front and center.

So, oldies and Mass help consume my weekends. Music, secular and religious, helps me understand the child I was and the man I have become!

Since January 24, 2011 ABC-FAMILY Channel has aired Sunday Mass 6:30 A.M. Eastern and Pacific time. The Mass is sponsored by the Passionist Order of Priests .

Sunday and daily Mass also is broadcast on EWTN each day at 8 A,M. Eastern time and is rebroadcast several times a day.

THE STANDING BOX

I was born with spastic cerebral palsy, the third oldest of nine children. This disability has taught me how to depend on others and trust in God with my daily needs. This childhood experience I am about to share showed me the importance of depending on God and those he has placed in my life. It is a lesson I have never forgotten!

Growing up in the 1950's and 60's children knew boundaries. If a child crossed those lines we understood there were real consequences. During one day in mid-September 1964, after testing my Mom's boundaries, I found out the costs of stepping over those limits firsthand.

In late June of that year I celebrated my tenth birthday. Summer was my least favorite season of the year; the heat and humidity bothers me. I also liked the structure of life once school started. Thus, I dreaded summer and in September I was glad school had started and never would have dreamed of missing a day of school due to constipation. Even at the age of ten, I sensed education would give me freedom. In our special education unit we had the basic reading, writing, and math as well as phonics. There were many others students like me who needed physical and/or speech therapy as well. Part of our physical therapy was to stand in the "Standing Box." There were some of us students that would spend half an hour to an hour each day, our leg braces locked at the knees in that box. While standing in the box we were able to do class assignments.

I especially liked to read or compose short stories while in the Standing Box. These activities helped me pass the time. I'd also liked to do word searches as well as crossword puzzles and often composed short stories on an IBM typewriter with a special key guard plate so fingers wouldn't strike the wrong key. As the Standing Box stretched my hamstrings, the reading, writing and word games stretched my mind.

Like many physically disabled people I've had bouts with constipation, at times not able to go for days sometime. When I was a child Mom or Dad had to give me what I called, "a poop bomb" or its official name a suppository.

I recall Mom awakening me early on that day at the beginning of the school-year of 1964-65. She said, "Billy, you haven't gone to the bathroom for days. It will be at least an hour before your brothers and sisters get up and so I'd like to give you a suppository now."

"No!" I flatly refused stating "I'll be fine." In truth I feared Mom placing something foreign up my butt.

Sensing my discomfort, she asked, "Would you like to stay home today? That way if you need to go, I can wipe your fanny."

Mom was not gentle about wiping rear ends or noses for that matter. It was not a pleasant thought and so I turned down Mom's offer. "Son, remember to ask Mrs. Barns (not her real name) if you have to go," she reminded as my wheelchair rolled onto the hydraulic lift of the school bus. It went without saying, given the options with which Mom had presented me, if I messed my pants that day, she would see to it her and I would have a long session later with her egg-turner to my bottom.

I made it to lunch without a problem. That's when I found Mom had set me up by filling my Superman thermos with prune juice. By mid-day I was dying, the prune juice doing its job. My rear began to rumble. I thought if I stayed in the wheelchair maybe I would be able to prevent an inevitable eruption in front of my classmates. As time drug on Mom's words came back to me, "If you need to go ask Mrs. Barns."

Mrs. Barns was the teacher's aide and a registered nurse. Still, being a ten-year-old at the time, I felt embarrassed about asking someone other than my family to wipe my bottom. Through the years I had prayed for constipation on various occasions. Especially during my annual four week stay at summer camp, sometimes able to put off having a BM only four times during my 28 day stay.

Therefore, on that early fall day of school I was quite confident I would succeed. I might have if our physical therapist, Mr. Ben Oak (not his real name), had not placed me in the Standing Box. It was about a 1:15, while the class was playing a word game, a game in which I generally excelled. But on that day I could not concentrate. I was very uncomfortable.

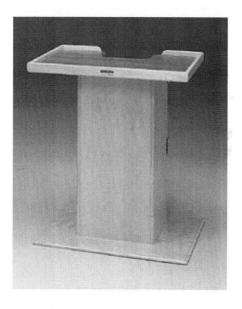

Our teacher wrote a long word on the blackboard, and we students had to write down as many words from that one word as possible. We wrote our lists on a yellow legal pad. Then, around 1:30, I erupted. I'd attempted to squeeze myself tight, but nothing could stop that volcano. Embarrassed, I whispered, telling Mrs. Barns what had happened.

Mrs. Barns phoned my folks, Mom woke my dad who had just come home from work and had gone to bed, and Dad came to pick me up in his station wagon. He was silent on the drive home. Thankfully, nothing leaked.

As Dad carried me into the house, I yelled out, "I am so sorry, Mommy." There was no response. Dad laid me down on the living room carpet to take off my braces and undress me. He then carried me to the bathroom.

When he'd finished bathing me, he got me into my Phillies pajamas; I proudly wore Jim Bunning's number 14 on my back. Dad wheeled me into the living-room for the family rosary, placing me on my stomach on the living room carpet and we began.

After we had finished this traditional Catholic form of prayer, before being put into bed, Mom wheeled me back into the bathroom and then sat down on the edge of the tub. At long last she spoke to me. Mom blamed herself for her not speaking up more forcefully that morning stating, "If I had smacked your ass this morning, insisted on that suppository, this mess could have been prevented."

After the lecture Mom lifted me from the wheelchair and while in mid-air lowered my Phillies pajamas to my ankles. I yelled, "No, Mommy!" Suffice to say, Mom warmed bottom with the egg turner. The one I tossed in the trash that morning. I am sure I received a few extra swats were given for me tossing the egg turner in the trash that morning.

As I began to fall asleep, I recalled the many times my Mom had reminded me, "By allowing others to help you, you help them to work out their salvation with God." But it was not until that early fall evening that the words sank in and I fully understood! The spanking brought the point home with no uncertainty. Never have I forgotten Mom's words; words which I have empowered me to ask for help when I need it; even if it is for something as personal as going to the bathroom. After all, I credit Mom's actions that day a big part of the reason I am able to live on my own today.

My parents are gone now, Dad died in March of 2001, Mom passed away in January of 2007. I've settled into an apartment complex that houses mainly low income senior citizens who are 65 years young and older. I am able to live here due to my disability. The apartment layout meets my special physical needs. I have an automatic push button door opener and care givers who help me tend to my daily needs. I gained some independence with my daily activities since my childhood. I am able to go shopping on my own, go to the theater, and doctors though I prefer company on these trips. I have gone from the standing box to therapy at a local YMCA. Use of a power-chair has made me more independent.

Between my parents, family and friends demonstrating Christian love, patience and understanding, I have been able to live a rather faith filled life.

A SMART MOUTH BOY
GETS HIS DUE

It was 1966. Like now, we were in an unpopular war, LBJ was President, the Baltimore Orioles swept the Los Angeles Dodgers in a four game series, the Boston Celtics beat the Los Angeles Lakers in the NBA Final 4 games to 3. And as for myself at that time, born in June of 1954 with spastic cerebral palsy, I was nothing but a smart mouth twelve-year-old.

On this particular day I recall Mom had just about enough with my flipped tongue. After all, I started early that morning and continued when I came home from school despite Mom's warning. "You aren't too old to take across my knee!"

Still, I was one never afraid to test the boundaries of my parents' limits. Why should this day be an exception? I took Mom's words as a personal challenge.

I responded without thinking. Though I mumbled the words, mom heard them, "I hope not or else you or Dad couldn't wipe my bottom." Mom was fuming. I knew the words were said in a very cruel and mean spirited fashion. Though the thought was provoked by a fear of mine that was genuine, Mom told me, "That thought, young man, is very insensitive." Thinking back on it, I'd have to agree!

Mom finished frying the potatoes for our home fries and cooking the chicken and vegetables for supper. There probably were canned peaches for dessert. Before we began each meal, we said grace as a family.

After dinner we gathered in the living room to pray the Rosary. A local radio station used to broadcast this prayer devotional in early evening throughout the week. Like grace each night we prayed the recitation of the Rosary as a family. Though as we got older several of us decided not to take part in this family prayer-ritual. At 12, I was almost at that age.

After we finished Mom said to me, "Smart mouth, now I wall tend to you." Within minutes Mom wheeled me in the bathroom. Before taking me out of my wheelchair Mom asked Dad, "When was the last time did Billy take a crap?"

Dad answered, "Three nights ago!" Without anymore discussion Dad brought in the hot water bag and contents for an enema. Mom began to empty the hot water bottle's contents into me.

I had been through this before. Constipation has been a recurring problem throughout my life due in part to my disability – spastic cerebral palsy and my limited mobility. My outer pants and underwear fall to floor. When the process was complete, mom sat me on the toilet. It seemed like a long time, but it was only 20-25 minutes before the enema began to complete its job. With a large family and one bathroom, I am sure it seemed like an eternity to everyone.

I called Dad, but Mom came in, before she spoke a word, I knew I was in trouble.

Mom came in stating, "You'll eat the words you threw at me this morning!" Mom warned me sternly. We were never abused. We simply learned boundaries and there were consequences for crossing them!

Trying to ease the tension I said sarcastically, "What are you going to do, spank my bottom?"

With that Mom turned me over as she sat on the tub's edge, placing me on her thighs, Mom wiped my butt. The toilet was clogged, it overflowed and I began to laugh due to being a bit nervous. Throughout my life, I've laughed when I am nervous. Psychologists refer to it as "a hangman's laugh." Mom went to the sink to wash her hands. Then Mom said, "I'm placing you back across my lap and will prove the point I was attempting to make this morning!" Nervously I said, "There is no need!" However, Mom was bound and determined this rite of childhood in 1950s and 1960s...

Though I continued to plead, it seemed that my

pleas fall on deaf ears

"Please, don't!" I begged one last time. Mom was not convinced as Mom yanked the belt from my pants which had been on the flooded bathroom floor. Before starting Mom put on the ceiling exhaust and centered me across her lap. That day as a 12- year-old smart mouth boy I really got my due. It was one of the last spankings of my childhood. Certainly it was the last I remember.

Like a long lost library book, Mom felt this spanking was long overdue!

And, who am I to say it wasn't?

TOPPING HER REWARD NIGHT WITH A SORE BOTTOM

It had been a long school year. It was May 2001. I had been teaching religious education to fourth and fifth graders for nine years at the time and in March of that year my Dad had died. Teaching to this point had been a distraction so, in truth, I dreaded the end of class school-year. In preparing for the second to last week, I had to select a male and female student of the year. My female student of the year was a no-brainer.

Peggy (not her real name) was one of my brightest students. Some of the students made fun of her due in part to her last name which they purposely butchered. She handled all this with great courage and not a word to those figuratively throwing darts at her.

Kids are often cruel. It was awards night as well as the week before the last night of class. Over the years I had rewarded a male and female student of the year. As such I gave a $10.00 gift certificate to Barnes & Noble in addition to their rewards. Thinking it was a nice gesture, I never expected such a response from her. As I handed this fifth-grader her reward and the gift-certificate, she didn't say thank you, but she asked me, "Why wasn't it $20?"

I thought to myself, perhaps saying it out loud, "You ungrateful brat, you need your bottom warmed!" Whether I spoke it out loud or not, her Dad thought the same thing. He took her by the hand and said to her, "Wait until you get home!"

The next week, the last week of class of the year Peggy told me in a thank you note:

> Daddy topped my award night off with a very sore bottom. I bought and read Charles Dickens' "Oliver Twist." By reading it and by working at a soup kitchen, Dad and Mom hope I will come to realize a deeper understanding of the plight of the poor.
>
> Thank you so much!
> Peggy

Equally important, Peggy's parents took her and her siblings shortly after that day to a soup kitchen. Week after week this family served their deprived brothers and sisters. This simple gesture became a weekly act of this family living out their Catholic faith. All things considered, I think I made a great choice naming her my female student of the year.

Hearing from this former student recently, this was affirmed. As I read her brief note, I was pleased to find out that this young woman is working toward a teaching degree. She hopes to touch the lives of children of the inner city, like many of those families Peggy and her family have touched since her youth.

Do I think she needed that paddling that day ten years ago this past May? I think combined with the community service, the book her family helped her choose as well as that spanking worked together as perfect medicine for an attitude adjustment. And the combination had awakened her to that reality.

Though Peggy probably will not earn as much as others in her field, in many respects her reward for the impact she could have on the lives of the students she teaches may be greater, than those who teach the rich. In my mind, that is of a much greater importance than any wealth she may not accumulate.

Like many who teach, she may become a hero to those who will be touched by her spirit and compassion for those in need.

Like Oliver Twist, all Peggy asked, that spring evening ten years that May evening was "Sir, could I have some more?" In the final analysis, I think that point could have been brought home without topping her reward night with a sore bottom!

In truth, as I've thought about it over time I think

the message could have been brought home without warming Peggy's bottom. The book as well as the visits to the soup-kitchen may have been all she needed to bring the stark reality of the plight of the poor to this bright young lady and truly changed her!

Like capital punishment, over the years, I have come to realize corporal punishment should be used sparingly. Both her Dad and I over-reacted to Peggy's remarks. They stung me, because I could not afford to give her or the other student a certificate of greater value. With that reality, I felt shame when she questioned me about the amount of the certificate. That reward night, over a decade ago, should have ended with a hug!

IN GOD'S ECONOMY

We can often get overwhelmed by those in need. Our mailboxes can be stuffed with heart wrenching details of the plight of this group or the other. We can have empathy for friends, and neighbors who may seem to be carrying heavy crosses in their lives; and wonder what we can do. This is especially true for those of us on a fixed income. Reaching out to others and supporting our parish community is a way of giving thanks to almighty God for what we have been given and what He has done for us.

The two main Scripture passages I will focus on throughout this feature hopefully drive home the point. The first passage is from the Gospel of Saint Luke. Though it is not mentioned, the woman in the story may have been embarrassed for being put on the spot.

In the four short verses of Saint Luke telling us her story we read of the poor widow's contribution. This poor woman placed two small coins in the collection plate. Jesus knows hearts and said, "I tell you truly that this poor widow put more in than all the rest; for those others have given from their surplus, while she has done so from her poverty" (Luke 21:1-4). In essence, this pious woman gave everything she had.

I paraphrased verses three and four to bring home the point. Time and again, God shows us that He multiplies our efforts. This is true in anything we do. Yet, we may need to be pushed into taking action. Nudged like the boy who gave five loaves and two fish. We may have to be put to task as those in the Temple that day the widow gave everything she had. As I said before Christ reads hearts.

Christ knew the woman understood that all she had was God's anyway. She and the young man had faith God would provide for their needs. Perhaps the woman in Luke's gospel knew it from her life experience.

For this widow may have gotten by with such help from some of the people from her faith community before. Nevertheless, her action as well as the young man's action in Matthew's Gospel spoke volumes to those present and to us today. It said to all who witness this display of her faith that this widow had confidence her needs would be met.

God wants us to give Him what we have. Recall the

time He multiplied the loaves and the fish given to Jesus by a boy in attendance (see Matthew 15:32-39). With the young man's contribution four thousand were fed that day, not counting women and children (verse 39).

God will not be out done in generosity. God can work miracles without us, but I know God prefers to do it with our help. Working with Him and through Him we can impact people's lives. When this happens, I believe God smiles. In God's economy, I think He expects it of us. Are we not called to be the arms, legs and feet of Christ for others?

For as Saint Francis said, "Live the Gospel always, when necessary use words." Each time we reach out to help someone in need we are fulfilling this command. This means to live the beatitudes (see St Matthew chapters 5-7).

Begin with prayer, asking God to show you a need and how you might help in the effort of an organization or individual to meet a goal. Our donation or contribution may seem like a drop in the bucket, but recall what was contributed by the poor widow mentioned earlier in this feature. Jesus made a big thing of it. We can derive from Christ's reaction that every contribution counts. Pray, consider where you've been fed spiritually and take action.

This means put feet to your words. It doesn't mean to contribute to every organization that asks for funds, but give to those charities or ministries or organization that have touched your life or someone you know. I choose personally to contribute to organizations that I or someone I know has or is being helped by.

A majority of my monthly tithing goes toward my parish and its outreaches. Local events can push one to assert our efforts to reach out to a particular institution. For instance, the recent death of a Deacon from our parish convinced me to make a monthly contribution in his name to the seminary in which he was trained. This monthly donation is also a way of thanking God for the countless Priests who have touched my life through the years. In light of this reality that God has shown me, the pledge may go beyond the year commitment.

For years, I have been touched by the witnesses of men and women on EWTN'S "The Journey Home." Both that program and the EWTN Radio program "Deep in Scripture" are sponsored by The Coming Home Network. After much prayer, I've decided to give regularly to The Coming Network. In doing so, I feel I am giving to ministries that feed me spiritually.

Although I am blessed to be able to attend weekly, I am grateful the Passionist Priests sponsor Mass on the ABC Family Channel at 6:30 a.m. eastern each Sunday, for I may not always have that privilege. The broadcast is also available anytime on the internet. Aside from that fact, Passionist Priests are great homilists in this writer's opinion.

Despite having a limited income, do you reach out to those in need or those ministries that have touched your live? I have! It is how I survive in God's economy it is how I am learning the joy and peace I have found through tithing. It has taking me years to come to this realization and become a joyful giver.

THE MAN UPSTAIRS

In late December of 2002 my Mom was hospitalized and had a heart bypass. Through June 11, 2003, when my Mom returned home my nephew Billy and I have lived alone in our family home. Seeing the range of emotions he went through I said to myself, "I am glad I am not that age!"

My nephew is a special man. At 21, he has uprooted his life and come to live with me, his 49-year-old uncle. I have seen the pain of a girl who broke his heart; and empathized with him as he shared his thoughts with me. I warned him as he went head on into another relationship with a girl who had hurt him before. I felt the pain of rejection several times in my own life.

I knew words couldn't mend the depth of the

sorrow he felt. So when I say in my house there's a man who lives upstairs, I can no longer say it with detachment; for I know the pain of unfulfilled love he has recently felt.

Therefore, I have an understanding of why he closes his door to his upstairs bedroom. By doing so he closes himself off to the world and to the real possibility of helping me if an emergency arises. He also closes himself from seeing my real need.

This thought frightens me. There are those who may ask "Why would I be scared?" Quite simply, I am disabled; I have spastic cerebral palsy and use a wheelchair for mobility. Like a parent is there to protect a child, this young man is here to protect me. For him, barely 21, it's an awesome responsibility.

And, he deserves much credit for taking on such a task. I know he's overwhelmed by other responsibilities, but his obligations to me are just as important. He has been a big part of the difference between me being placed in a nursing home facility or living at home. I am grateful for that fact, but I hate the hours of isolation, due to his busy schedule.

Nevertheless, too often due to his daily agenda, I feel very much alone. Like my relationship with God at times I feel distant from this young man. And yet, the time I mentioned about his struggle with unfulfilled love is an example of times that have made us close.

The experience has given me a deeper understanding of the word tolerance. The young man and I have learned much through living with one another.

We have also gained a great deal respect for one another. I have come to know he is a hard worker and I have learned to tolerate, if not appreciate his music.

Although, we've had our differences this young man has made me stretch my horizons as few people have done in my life. I have felt great personal satisfaction in what I have accomplished through his presence over the last half year. He remains here, though my mom is now home. I am glad. For I dreaded seeing this time nearing its end.

Much of the time he helped me, he did so without pay. Due to his hectic schedule it took him many months to do the paperwork needed to get paid by the state for services he gave to me. He was proud of the work boots he bought with money he earned from his first paycheck from working for me. I felt satisfied that I made a difference in his life. I know he's made a difference in mine!

Thank you, William Walter Langan, I know this time we've had together has been a gift from the "Man Upstairs."

SAINT MAXIMILIAN KOLBE

The most deadly poison of our times is indifference. And this happens, although the praise of God should know no limits. Let us strive, therefore, to praise Him to the greatest extent of our powers.

I am part Polish and part Irish. So I was bubbling with pride the day Maximilian Kolbe, a Polish priest, was canonized by Blessed John Paul II. The date was October 10, 1982. Kolbe's ethnicity aside, I was also drawn to him because he was a gifted journalist.

As Pope Paul II was being declared Blessed by the Church in May of 2011, I was drawn back to that day in October 1982 when I heard the news. Among the people he elevated to saint on that day was a humble priest who gave his life for another.

Born January 8, 1894, our hero was given the name Raymond at baptism. He took the name Maximilian as his name in religion, as a member of the Franciscan order. The words I quoted at the top of this article are his. They could have been penned yesterday, about our times. They were words of a humble priest, a servant of God who gave his life so that another man could live. Incarcerated in 1941 at Auschwitz, the Nazi death camp, Maximilian Kolbe took literally the words of Saint John's Gospel: "Greater love has no man than this that a man lay down his life for his friends" (John 15:13). When another man was condemned — a family man with children — Maximilian offered to die in his place.

After many days of slow starvation in a stifling bunker, the priest was finished off with a lethal injection. The day of his death, August 14, is now his Feast Day.

Tears of joy and pride came to my eyes the day this priest and martyr was declared a saint. "The Saint of Auschwitz" was ordained in 1918. Since his youth Kolbe had a great devotion to Mary, the Mother of God. A visit to a shrine in his childhood changed his life direction. The Blessed Virgin appeared to him and asked which cup would young Raymond prefer, **"the cup of purity or that of a martyr?"** He responded, "Both."

Our Blessed Mother lovingly responded, "Then you shall drink them both!" Thus she indicated the kind of life and the type of death he would experience. Kolbe underwent a type of martyrdom that John Paul II himself could have faced, if circumstances had altered slightly on many given days of the Nazi occupation. So, I am certain the Holy Father identified strongly with this priest from his homeland.

In 1971 Pope Paul VI had beatified Maximilian, the next-to-last step on the way to public proclamation of sainthood. On that occasion Pope Paul urged the Church and its people to ask for Kolbe's intercession. He called the man a "Martyr of Love."

The Church has put Maximilian forth as a model and patron for prisoners. He served prisoners by hearing Confessions and offering Mass for them to the end. The prayer below is for intercession on behalf of prisoners. The prayer is powerful!

Prisoner's Prayer to Saint Maximilian Kolbe

O Prisoner-Saint of Auschwitz,
Help me in my plight
Introduce me to Mary, the Immaculata,
Mother of God. She prayed for Jesus in
A Jerusalem jail. She prayed for you
In a Nazi prison camp. Ask her to comfort
Me in my confinement. May she teach me
always to be good.
If I am lonely, may she say "God is here."
If I feel hate, may she say "God is love."
If I am tempted, may she say "God is pure."

If I sin, may she say "God is mercy."
If I am in darkness, may she say "God is light."
If I am unjustly condemned, may she say "God is truth."
If I have pain in soul or body, may she say "God is peace."
If I lose hope, may she say: "God is with you all days, and so am I."
Amen.

In introducing you to two Christian heroes of mine, true friends of Mary, the Mother of God, I pray you are inspired to read more about their lives: both *Saint Maximilian Kolbe,* as well as John Paul II who was named a Blessed of the Church. I know I will be inspired.

A LOST ART

Letter writing has become a lost art. Instead of penning a letter we too often seem to be too busy to put down our thoughts on paper in a constructive way. Using complete sentences and showing someone you thought of them enough to send them something personal takes time and thought.

A well written letter takes time to create. While contemplating about what one wants to say to an individual we dash off a quick e-mail with little thought behind it. Instead of taking two or three days before placing one's thoughts on paper to the individuals or family members to which we are communicating with.

At times we send thoughts electronically while they are still raw. I am as guilty as anyone else. However, when I allow myself the time to envision what I want to convey to the person prior to putting pen to paper or more accurately, in my case, my hands to my computer keyboard my true meaning is more likely to be understood.

Like a sculptor's use of marble and a chisel as tools of their craft; words well written or spoken by a gifted speaker, letter writer or author each can set a tone for communication that says welcome, thank you or I am here for you.

The letter can be short, but nonetheless, for the greatest impact it must state its directive from its onset. Once the letter's points are made wrap it up with a power punch, re-stating the correspondence or speech's main purpose.

Recently I have written letters for various reasons that included family members and friends: a welcome to an incoming pastor, a farewell to a retiring priest, a line of thanks, and for continued encouragement.

Excerpts from these bring home the point. Each example is self explanatory. I open the first to a cousin with a tone of guilt, but conclude the portion of the passage using humor. Some examples are below:

> It has been just over six months since I've written. Your Mom put us all through quite a scare. I hope things stay stable for awhile. Your mother has been in my thoughts and prayers. I remembered her at Mass this morning.
>
> When I spoke to her last week, she said,

"Haven't asked anyone to get me cigarettes."
Based on my conversation with you, I find that
hard to believe! How about you?

I end it "Love and prayers," and sign my name. In
this simple note I let my cousin know I am there for
her. My signature also means a great deal. The
signature tells an individual whether handwritten or
type the author took time to personalize the note. Like
a Hallmark card, the person "cared enough to send
their very best."

I had been writing a letter in a spirit of
thanksgiving to our pastor, who was retiring for many
weeks. I had written and rewritten the letter in my
head many times; however, I didn't put my thoughts
to paper until the morning of his farewell mass and
reception. The words were heartfelt.

How can I thank you for the doors you have
opened for me and so many others in this parish
as well as in this community? You have led
with love and compassion for all. I am saddened
by your departure, but know you must move on.
I will miss your sermons which came from
your vast life experiences and love of reading. I
pray God gives you many years of serving the
Spanish community.

I ended the brief note with the salutation "all the
best." I had let this compassionate shepherd know
what he meant to me and our parish community time

and again.

In like fashion, I wrote a letter of welcome to the new pastor. It was essentially a note pledging my support to him. I opened the letter with this introduction:

> I have been a lifetime parishioner of Saint Michael the Archangel Church and look forward to serving the parish community in whatever way I possibly can. Born with spastic cerebral palsy, I am the third oldest of nine children and will turn 52 next month.
>
> My parents were founding members of the parish. Married in 1948, they moved to Levittown in 1953.

After a paragraph in which I spoke about my Dad's death, I wrote of my Mom as I completed the note to our new pastor with these words and letter sign-off:

> Mom still lives in the home in which we grew up. I lived there until last August. Two of her grandsons live there now. Mom will turn 80 in January. I visit her at least once a week. She is a woman of faith.
>
> Look forward to serving the parish under your leadership.
>
> In the love of Jesus and Mary,...

Bob Rooney, the father of a good friend of mine, wrote me a great critique of the feature you are reading. Towards the end of his comments he states simply the following thought:

> If Thomas Jefferson, or John and Abigail Adams had written E-mail we would have lost a great and wonderful look into the lives of our country's founders. The letter we write today may give insight to those who come after us. E-mail is ephemeral, paper may survive. We can only hope that letter writing does not become a lost art.

It has been my hope that this column has given readers a new appreciation in the lost art of letter writing. Hopefully, it challenges some to put pen to paper, writing inspired words that touch someone's heart today!

A DAY OF BLESSINGS

It was Friday, April 12th. I had picked up my new glasses at 11 a.m. the day before. Still, today I realize I'll have to take them back to where they were purchased for an adjustment. The eyewear keeps falling off my nose. My attendant wheeled me over to the doctor's office. I am grateful the predicted rain didn't materialize. We would have had to make other arrangements or pick then up another day. However it wouldn't have mattered. To get all that needs to be done in a day, one must often go with the flow.

I smile at God's timing. My attendant quickly washed and dressed me and the two of us were on our way. It would take us 45 minutes. The return trip would only take 35 minutes. Gabriel, my attendant noted, "It is easier to push down hill!" This Godsend from Haiti has been there for me for over eight and a half years; as of this moment in the summer of 2009.

The next day a friend who works for me on weekends and has been there for me in times of emergency walked beside me to morning Mass. I like Saturdays, because my day usually begins and ends with Mass and reception of Holy Communion. Despite anything else that happened during the day - the Mass and the Eucharist make the burdens of the day easier to bear.

When we come back from Mass I must ask this young man to help me on the toilet. And, yes, when I'm finished the man wipes my bottom. This friend doesn't complain. His help at this moment is an act of God's grace which shows through him. Though, I am a man of 53, this need makes me feel like a child of three about to get spanked as I bend over to get wiped. For me, it is one of the most humiliating parts of the day.

For lunch I have a pork chop, mixed vegetables and apple sauce that are part of a meal that is given to me by a group called Aid For Friends. It is coordinated with the help of various churches and denominations including the local Catholic Parishes. Every time I eat one of their homemade meals, I ask God to bless those who share of their bounty or perhaps of their want. For we don't know the life circumstances of those that contribute meals or give of their time to deliver them.

I eat these prepared meals at lunch due in part to the fact that someone is there to help me cook those meals. I also don't like to go bed with a heavy stomach.

Upon retuning from the Saturday Vigil Mass, I have a surprise visit from my sister Rosemary and her husband Mike. Their visit means I won't have to wait until after ten that evening to get in bed. Mike helps me transfer from my power chair to my hospital bed.

As I reflect on the day about to end, I am amazed at the number of people who have directly or indirectly impacted my life today. For that matter whom I may have made an impact on myself.

I know two young girls have recently become pen pals. It is great that they share so easily about their faith and lives. I hope their fire doing so never dies. One of those wrote me about a book on early martyrs of the Church including Saint Agnes. "The book was a wonderful read written by Cardinal Wiseman."

With an endorsement like that who could resist from picking it and adding it to their summer must read list. With youth on fire for Our Blessed Lord like the two young ladies I am speaking of how could I help but think of days such as these anything but a blessing!

A THANKFUL HEART

Thanksgiving is my favorite holiday. It reminds me to take stock in how God has blessed me and how I am obligated to give back. Yes, indeed, mine is a thankful heart. One who knows God has protected me from myself at times as well as others who would do harm to me. He is indeed a God of mercy.

I am thankful for family and friends. They are the strings, unsung heroes that allow me to be a living witness for Christ. Life without them would be empty, void of purpose. I am grateful I am a people person and need others around me. I am thankful I am not a monk for in my heart I know I could not handle the isolation.

I am grateful this American feast has not become as commercialized as Christmas. This fact keeps this holiday's sacredness. It is a holiday where Americans celebrate the Domestic Church; the family with its good points as well as blemishes. This holiday is a feast in which we show gratitude for all that we have been given. Beyond its food and customs thankfulness is at the heart of this special feast's celebration.

I love to begin Thanksgiving morning by attending Mass. The Eucharistic Liturgy truly is one of the highlights of my day. It is a way of showing my thankfulness to God. The Mass is a reminder of God's love for us. He comes to us body, blood, soul and divinity at every Mass.

I am thankful God has given me the ability to speak for those who can't speak or choose not to speak, the marginalized of our society; the elderly, the disabled and unborn. When defending them, I pray God gives me the words to say. This charge is an awesome responsibility. One for which I am most grateful God helps me carry out for I could not do it alone. A thankful heart is one ready to give. A heart beaming with gratitude can impact the world around them.

As Thanksgiving approaches think of someone who has been your mentor. Remind them what they have meant to you and your success. Show them you have a thankful heart by teaching what you have learned to others.

In essence a thankful heart allows an individual to live the Beatitudes. A thankful heart allows an individual to take up his cross everyday following

Christ to Calvary. Though Simon was a reluctant servant who aided in carrying Christ's cross, Jesus is more than willing to help us carry our own. In times of struggle I have asked him for such aid.

Lastly, I am thankful God will not scorn a contrite heart. I am grateful I have to look no further than to see own my sinfulness as to see why Christ came. With such awareness how can I judge others? I don't go to church to prove my holiness, but, to acknowledge my total dependency on God!

For these and so many other reasons, mine is thankful heart. Have a blessed Thanksgiving.

IN THANKSGIVING

How God Answered My Prayer for Healing

In September of 1998, I had written an article entitled "But I Asked to Be Healed" (read article here) was published in New Covenant magazine. In that article, I examined various healings recorded in Sacred Scripture that Jesus had performed, but I looked at them from a unique perspective: that view from the eyes of someone who has a physical disability. As a man with spastic cerebral palsy—I use a wheelchair for mobility—I have always been deeply moved by these stories.

I can honestly say that the reflection and self-examination that was necessary to complete the feature changed my life! I no longer ask, "Why can't I be healed?" The truth is that I have met so many wonderful people as a result of my disability, whether I get cured or not now seems insignificant. I still love to read about the miracles of Christ, but now I see how often the healing was connected with forgiveness. In place of asking for a physical healing, these days I ask for the ability to live the challenge Jesus gave us in the "Our Father."

For me, that challenge is to refrain from judging the nine lepers who did not come back to thank Jesus for healing them (see Lk. 17:11–19). I used to be critical of the cured lepers that did not give thanks, but then I thought, "How many times have I rushed out of Mass without proper reflection? How many times have I thoughtlessly spoken in less than a whisper, forgetting that Christ is in the tabernacle? Did I not display a sign of being as ungrateful as those nine lepers who did not give thanks?"

Today, I am still critical, not so much at others, but at my own motives for doing things. As I reread the story published in September of 1998, I see a young woman, Nancy, mentioned in the feature. As I recall, she was the real reason I went to the prayer meeting; I wanted to impress her more than I wanted to honor God. Today I realize what God did through her.

A Look Back

When I met Nancy back in September of 1979, I would have followed her anywhere. She was a dynamic young Catholic woman who was actively involved in the Newman Center at a nearby college, and I was a "cradle Catholic" who, prior to that time, only lived my faith on Sundays. One afternoon, as we were leaving the Newman Center together, Nancy asked me if I wanted to go to a prayer meeting with her later that evening at St. Agnes Church. I gave a resounding "yes!" (As one can see, my motives weren't the highest at the time, but God worked with that just the same.)

As a few of Nancy's friends carried me up several flights of stairs that night, I was sure I knew what the paralytic from Luke 5:17–26 must have felt when he was carried up to the top of that house to be lowered through the roof. I could almost hear his friends saying, "If this doesn't work, we'll break our backs for nothing." Indeed, this is exactly what Nancy's friends were saying as they carried me.

I wasn't healed that night.

A Deeper Healing

I used to empathize with those men and the paralytic in the story, feeling that if I weren't healed, all of this would be for nothing. Hogwash! I now know that if God had healed me that night, I may have won Nancy over. Instead, over a short period of time, this remarkable young woman and the students and staff of the Newman Center won me over for Christ and His Church. This woman got me to attend daily Mass and receive Jesus daily in the Eucharist. Through her efforts, as well as those of the Holy Spirit, my view of God was transformed from an angry God, to a God rich in mercy.

I wasn't healed that night, at least not in the way I was expecting. I did not get what I wanted, but I have come to the point where I now want what God wants for me. And that, my friends, have been the core of a true spiritual healing.

Jesus heals people. And the stories of miracles have always lifted my spirits. For so many years, the desire to be healed was so deep in my heart. Today, I realize how God answered that prayer.

In my original article, I concluded with a prayer for those of us who have visible crosses. However, our God is the God of all. Therefore, I feel it is a must to include all of us, who live with crosses both visible and invisible. May all of us who are in the Body of Christ realize this: "On him lies a punishment that brings us peace, and through his wounds we are healed" (Is. 53:5).

"YOU ARE A PRIEST FOREVER..."

The month of May reminds me to pray for Priests. Part of the reason is the fact that Ordination in the Philadelphia Archdiocese of its Priests takes place. Pope John Paul II was Ordained November 1, 1946. It was amazing to me that despite his position I, and I am sure others could see that this humble man had the heart of a parish Priest. His spirit reminded me so much of John the XXIII. Pope John Paul II became pope October 16, 1978; fittingly, one of the two months of the year the Church sets aside for Mary, the Mother of God.

The late pope often stated "Without priests there would be no Eucharist." Mary had the privilege to give birth to Christ once while priests can do it at each Mass they serve. Is there any wonder priests that stay close to Mary have a great devotion to Jesus in the Eucharist? I think not.

Like John XXIII Pope John Paul II worked tirelessly for World peace. John XXIII helped prevent a world disaster by his intervention during The Cuban Missile Crisis and Pope John Paul II's effort to "bring down the wall." Both men earned Time Magazine's "Man of the Year." John XXIII was given the award months before his death. A biographical feature by Father Richard Schiblin, "Pope John XXIII, Preacher of Peace" in the *Liguorian* magazine, quoted John XXIII:

"I beg heads of state not to remain insensitive to the cry of humanity: Let them do all in their power to save peace."

The statement was issued October 26, 1962 by the Vatican and on the 28th the missiles were removed and disaster was adverted.

This Pope who oversaw the opening session of the Vatican II Council did not live to see its completion. Of the Missile Crisis and other pending disasters the Pope hoped world leaders "looked to the relations of nations as a beginning point for peace" (February 2010 *Liguorian* Magazine). Though he couldn't travel much, John XXIII, had a huge impact on the world. He died June 3, 1963.

An article speaking of John XXIII efforts to prevent the Soviet Union and the States from war stated of the Pope's challenge for cooler heads to prevail:

John XXIII ... made an unusual foray into contemporary politics during the Cuban Missile Crisis of 1962. With the United States and the Soviet Union on the brink of nuclear war, John made an impassioned plea over the Vatican Radio: "We beg all rulers not to be deaf to the cry of humanity." This may have played a role in Nikita Krushchev's decision to back down, because it could have allowed him to do so without entirely losing face.

John Paul II was known as the traveling Pope, and John XXIII stated in his autobiography "Journal of a Soul" that he "felt imprisoned by the walls of the Vatican and longed to travel." John XXIII must have felt isolated by his position. In truth, age and the state of world travel both played a factor in this aged leader of the Catholic Church feeling that way.

Despite these factors and dying of cancer he called an ecumenical council. His efforts started a "New Pentecost" within the Church. One can still see the ripple effects of that Council today. With his insight and willingness to listen to prompting of the Holy Spirit he allowed the laity to have a much greater role than prior to this historical Council.

John XXIII didn't live to see the work of the Council complete; however, his vision allowed the Mass to be said in one's own vernacular instead of just being said in Latin. The priest also at Mass no longer had his back to the congregation. When these changes were implemented I felt closer to God and

His Church. If the language had not changed, I may not have remained Catholic as an adult. This said there is beauty to a Eucharistic Liturgy done in Latin.

If Pope John XXIII is best known as a peacemaker than John Paul II legacy has to his love of the world youth, his love of travel and his willingness to elevate men and women of all walks of life to sainthood.

One of those saints John Paul II named was Saint Maximilian Kolbe. The date was October 10, 1982. Several years ago I penned an article about that day and my pride in my Polish/Irish heritage. I began the feature by quoting the saint:

"The most deadly poison of our times is indifference. And this happens, although the praise of God should know no limits. Let us strive, therefore, to praise Him to the greatest extent of our powers."

IN A DAY OF
CELEBRATION

There are milestone days in our lives we celebrate with family and friends. They are watershed days in our lives; important days in our faith journey. They include Baptisms, First Holy Communions, graduations or a wedding day or special anniversaries such as Silver or Golden like the one celebrated in May of 2005.

A Golden Anniversary was the reason for celebrating in May of that year. The date was Saturday, May 28, 2005. Friends of mine were making merry celebrating 50 years of marriage.

Like 50 years earlier, their special occasion began with a Mass and Eucharist surrounded by family and friends as the couple affirmed their love and commitment to one another once again. On this day of celebration, I felt truly blessed.

Becoming good friends over the last few years, I was very glad to just be a part of their special day. Indeed I was honored to be considered among the friends invited to this festive event. Yes, I felt truly blessed.

Frank worked many years as a public school teacher. He also worked part-time many years for J.C. Penney along with other jobs. The impact of ripples he had on lives of others particularly are im-measurable. This was but another reason I was honored to be there, considered among the friends invited to this festive event. Yes, I felt truly blessed.

Likewise, Pat has had her own impact on others. For many years she ran an in-home-day-care. Countless parents and guardians were able to go to work and provide for their families as a result of her efforts. This was but another reason I was honored to be there, considered among the friends invited to this festive event. Yes, I felt truly blessed.

What happened in May of 1955? For one thing, I was only 11 months old, "Damn Yankees" hit Broadway and the Brooklyn Dodgers were at the start of a season in which they won it all. But, on this day of celebration, we are recalling one event; the marriage of Pat and Frank. For this reason, I felt truly blessed.

To recall the day I first made a ripple in their lives is to go back to a day several years ago when Frank fell faint as he lectored at Mass one weekend. I sought Pat out, told her Frank was in my prayers and gave her my telephone number sparking a friendship. So, on this day of celebration, I felt truly blessed.

Since the day we met we have been welcomed into each others homes for prayer, food, tears and laughter. We have told stories, enriched our faith and our lives through one another's presence. Friends bring out the best in each other. Friends are there for one another in good times and bad. Yes, on this day of celebration, I felt truly blessed.

I met a woman who was a baby sitter for Frank and Pat's children. This woman lives in a town I only pass through. In an afternoon of conversation I realized I met a woman whose family was a part of the town's genesis. Yes, on this occasion, I felt truly blessed.

With pride in her voice and a gleam in her eyes I was informed that next to the restaurant where the celebration took place was built a hotel crafted by the woman's grandfather whom I sat with throughout the afternoon. He also built the town's bank. In dining with this sixty-year-old woman, Betty, in her presence, I felt truly blessed.

Along life's journey, we meet many people, the pebbles we throw to touch their lives we hope have a positive ripple or impact. Perhaps that impact can make a day of loneliness, a day of celebration; a day they are truly blessed a bit more special!

My prayer is that I did this for Betty, who asked me to come and say a few words. I hope Frank and Pat were not disappointed. For me, Betty's storytelling made this day of celebration memorable. I hope these words spoken from the heart have made this occasion richer for those present here today!

Made in the USA
Lexington, KY
25 November 2012